COMMON CORE

MATH

Activities that Captivate, Motivate, & Reinforce

Kindergarten

by Jill Norris

IncentivePublications

BY WORLD BOOK

a Scott Fetzer company

Illustrated by Kathleen Bullock
Cover by Penny Laporte
Edited by Marjorie Frank

Print Edition ISBN 978-1-62950-193-2
E-book Edition ISBN 978-1-62950-194-9 (PDF)

World Book, Inc.
233 North Michigan Avenue
Suite 2000
Chicago, Illinois 60601
U.S.A.

For information about World Book and Incentive Publications products, call **1-800-967-5325,** or visit our websites at **www.worldbook.com** and **www.incentivepublications.com.**

Printed in the United States of America by Sheridan Books, Inc.
Chelsea, Michigan
1st printing August 2015

CONTENTS

Operations and Algebraic Thinking

Number and Operations in Base Ten

Measurement and Data

Geometry

Reproducible Manipulatives and Aids

Assessment and Answer Keys

Great Support for
Common Core State Standards!

Invite your students to enjoy delightful dinosaurs (and learn some dinosaur facts) as they develop strong foundations for understanding math concepts. Young mathematicians will enjoy the engaging dinos and their friends, manipulating them around a swamp or behind a rock as they discuss and solve math problems.

This is more than a paper-pencil book. It includes the manipulatives, storyboards, games, and open-ended questions that will encourage meaningful discussion and analytical thinking. For each of the Kindergarten Common Core State Standards for Mathematics, you will find targeted, hands-on activities, opportunities for students to talk about strategies they use to solve the problems, and a chance to create and solve new problems.

Math Talk

"Math talk" is a critical component of math instruction and learning for kindergartners. Make time every day for some math talk. You'll notice that many of the activities in this book provide time and ways for students to talk about the math ideas and processes that they are using. These math talks can reveal a student's understanding or misunderstanding; encourage students to identify patterns in the number system; and support the development of deeper reasoning, language, and social skills.

To inspire math talk:

- Encourage students to think about and verbalize what a problem is asking.
- Prompt them to think about and describe a strategy they could use to solve the problem (in addition to determining an answer). Encourage multiple possibilities for strategies. When students share their strategies with others, they learn to clarify and express their thinking, thereby developing mathematical language.
- Challenge students to explain what they are thinking, make connections, look for relationships, and identify similarities and differences between problems.

Using Manipulatives

Many activities in this book make use of counters, number lines, cutout shapes, flash cards, cards to sort, tangram-like pieces, and other items to handle, move, count, and inspire problem solving. Such objects are integral to the learning of math concepts for young students. A section of reproducible pages in the back of the book provides many of these items. However, your use of items for students to handle need not be limited to these. Like "math talk," the "doing" of math (by moving and manipulating objects to create and solve problems) helps students grasp and integrate the deep understandings of concepts at the heart of the kindergarten standards.

Reproduce the manipulatives (pages 108-130) on card stock or sturdy paper. You might laminate some or all of these. Work with these concrete models to build numbers and to figure out computation problems until students no longer need them. Many activities include a **materials list** so you will know what manipulatives are essential. The materials list specifies the materials required for a student or pair of students, unless otherwise noted.

How to Use This Book

The pages are tools to support your teaching of the concepts, processes, and skills outlined in the Common Core State Standards. This is not a curriculum; it is a collection of engaging experiences for you to use with your students.

- The text on the pages is meant to be read to the students by an adult. Pages are not intended solely for independent work. With adult involvement, work in a large group or small group setting to deepen understandings and apply skills to new situations.

- The book is organized according to the Common Core math domains. Use the tables on pages 12-16 and the label at the bottom corner of each activity page to identify the standards category supported by that page.

- Although each activity is focused on a particular standard, many build on one another and require that a student has an understanding of the skills introduced and practiced in prior activities.

- Use any given page to introduce, explain, teach, practice, extend, assess, provide independent work, start a discussion about, or get students collaborating on a skill or concept.

- Have manipulatives ready for each activity. These are found on pages 108-130. (See page 8 information about reproducible manipulatives.) See the materials lists on many of the pages.

- Model playing the games and using record pages before expecting students to use them independently. A pair of students can demonstrate the game as you guide them. The other class members can practice filling out the record sheet for one of the players.

- Some pages (such as pages 19, 22, and 121-124) include factual information about dinosaurs. Your students will enjoy learning about the dinosaurs as they build math understanding. As you discuss the information, use the facts to compare attributes of the dinosaurs.

- Always review and discuss the work together. Encourage students to share a variety of problem-solving techniques. Here are some ways kindergartners explained strategies they used or could use to solve the addition problem, 7 + 5 = ___.

Use a ten-frame. Put in seven counters. Get five more counters. Fill up the ten-frame. You have two counters. That means you have ten ones and two left over, or twelve.

I know seven and three make ten. I think in my head, "Five is two plus three." So I put the three with the seven and have two left over. Ten and two more are twelve.

I know that seven plus seven equals fourteen. I know that five is two less than seven. So seven plus five is two less than fourteen.

You could use real things like counters or buttons. Get seven and five more, then count them.

You could borrow someone's fingers. You hold up seven and your friend holds up five. Count the fingers.

You could use the number line. Start with seven and count on five more spaces.

I know that five plus five equals ten. Since seven is two more than five, I added two to the answer and got twelve.

About Common Core State Standards for Mathematics

The Common Core State Standards for Mathematics seek to expand conceptual understanding of the key ideas of math while they strengthen foundational skills, operations, and principles. They identify what students should know, understand, and be able to do—with an emphasis on explaining principles and applying them to a wide range of situations. To best help students gain and master these robust standards for math . . .

1. Know the standards well. Keep them in front of you. Understand for yourself the big picture of what the standards seek to do. Unpack them, rephrase the standards in "kid-friendly" language, and share them with your students. (See www.corestandards.org)

2. Work to apply, expand, and deepen student skills. With activities in this book (or any learning activities), plan to include

   . . . interaction with peers in pairs, small groups, and large groups

   . . . plenty of discussion, integration, and hands-on work with math concepts

   . . . emphasis on questioning, analyzing, modeling math situations, explaining what the students are doing and thinking, using tools effectively, and applying what the students are doing and learning to real world problems

   . . . lots of observation, meaningful feedback, follow-up, and reflection

3. Ask such questions as these to encourage sharing and clarify thinking:
   - *What does this ask you to do?*
   - *How did you see it?*
   - *Who would like to share your thinking?*
   - *How did you figure it out?*
   - *What did you do first?*
   - *What did you do next?*
   - *How did you think about that?*
   - *Who else used this strategy to solve the problem?*
   - *What strategies do you see being used?*
   - *Which strategies seem to work best for this problem?*
   - *Could there be another answer?*
   - *How can you show that your answer is right?*
   - *What does this remind you of?*
   - *What patterns do you notice?*
   - *Where have you seen this in real life?*

Standards for Mathematical Practice

St. #	Standard	Pages in This Book that Support the Standard
MP1	Make sense of problems and persevere in solving them.	18-42, 44-68, 70-78-80-88, 90-106
MP2	Reason abstractly and quantitatively.	18-42, 44-68, 70-78-80-88, 90-106
MP3	Construct viable arguments and critique the reasoning of others.	26, 30, 36, 37, 40, 41-42, 44, 45, 47, 50, 55, 56, 57, 58, 66, 67, 68, 80, 81, 82, 83, 84, 86, 87, 88, 95
MP4	Model with mathematics.	18-42, 44-68, 70-78-80-88, 90-106
MP5	Use appropriate tools strategically.	18-42, 44-68, 70-78-80-88, 90-106
MP6	Attend to precision.	18-42, 44-68, 70-78-80-88, 90-106
MP7	Look for and make use of structure.	19, 23, 24, 30, 31, 32, 33, 38, 39, 40, 41-42, 46, 48, 60, 61, 70, 71, 72, 73, 74, 75, 76, 77, 78, 83, 84, 85, 86, 87, 88, 92, 93, 94, 95, 96, 97, 98, 99, 100, 101, 102, 103, 104, 105, 106
MP8	Look for and express regularity in repeated reasoning.	21, 22, 23, 28, 30, 31, 32, 33, 34, 35, 36, 37, 38, 39, 40, 41-42, 49, 50, 51, 52, 53, 54, 55, 56, 57, 58, 70, 71, 72, 73, 74, 75, 76, 77, 78, 80, 81, 82, 83, 84, 85

Kindergarten Common Core State Standards for Mathematical Content

K.CC   Counting and Cardinality

St. #	Standard	Pages in This Book that Support the Standard
Know number names and the count sequence.		
K.CC.A.1	Count to 100 by ones and tens.	18, 19, 20, 21, 22, 23, 24, 25, 28, 29, 30, 31, 32, 33, 34, 35, 36, 37, 38, 39, 30, 41, 42
K.CC.A.2	Count forward beginning from a given number within the known sequence (instead of having to begin at 1).	21, 22, 23, 24
K.CC.A.3	Write numbers from 0 to 20. Represent a number of objects with a written numeral 0-20 (with 0 representing a count of no objects).	25, 26, 27, 28, 29, 30, 31, 32, 33, 34, 35, 36, 37, 38, 39, 40, 41, 42
Count to tell the number of objects.		
K.CC.B.4	Understand the relationship between numbers and quantities; connect counting to cardinality.	28, 29, 30, 31, 32, 33, 34, 35, 36, 37, 38, 39, 40, 41, 42
K.CC.B.4.A	When counting objects, say the number names in the standard order, pairing each object with one and only one number name and each number name with one and only one object.	27, 28, 29, 30, 31, 32, 33, 34, 35, 36, 37
K.CC.B.4.B	Understand that the last number name said tells the number of objects counted. The number of objects is the same regardless of their arrangement or the order in which they were counted.	34, 35, 36, 37, 38, 49, 40, 41, 42
K.CC.B.4.C	Understand that each successive number name refers to a quantity that is one larger.	34, 35, 36, 37, 38, 49, 40, 41, 42
K.CC.B.5	Count to answer "how many?" questions about as many as 20 things arranged in a line, a rectangular array, or a circle, or as many as 10 things in a scattered configuration; given a number from 1-20, count out that many objects.	37, 38, 39, 40, 41, 42

Counting and cardinality standards continue on the next page.

Kindergarten Common Core State Standards for Mathematical Content

K.CC   Counting and Cardinality, continued

St. #	Standard	Pages in This Book that Support the Standard
Compare numbers.		
K.CC.C.6	Identify whether the number of objects in one group is greater than, less than, or equal to the number of objects in another group, e.g., by using matching and counting strategies. (Use groups of up to 10 objects.)	38, 39, 40, 41, 42
K.CC.C.7	Compare two numbers between 1 and 10 presented as written numerals.	24, 25, 38, 39, 40, 41, 42

K.OA   Operations and Algebraic Thinking

St. #	Standard	Pages in This Book that Support the Standard
Understand addition, and understand subtraction.		
K.OA.A.1	Represent addition and subtraction with objects, fingers, mental images, drawings, sounds (e.g., claps), acting out situations, verbal explanations, expressions, or equations.	44, 45, 46, 47, 48, 59, 50, 51, 52, 53, 54, 55, 56, 57, 58, 59, 60, 61, 62, 63, 64, 65, 66, 67, 68
K.OA.A.2	Solve addition and subtraction word problems, and add and subtract within 10, e.g., by using objects or drawings to represent the problem.	44, 45, 46, 47, 48, 59, 50, 51, 52, 53, 54, 55, 56, 57, 58, 59, 60, 61, 62, 63, 64, 65, 66, 67, 68
K.OA.A.3	Decompose numbers less than or equal to 10 into pairs in more than one way, e.g., by using objects or drawings, and record each decomposition by a drawing or equation (e.g., 5 = 2 + 3 and 5 = 4 + 1).	56, 57, 58, 59, 60, 61
K.OA.A.4	For any number from 1 to 9, find the number that makes 10 when added to the given number, e.g., by using objects or drawings, and record the answer with a drawing or equation.	58, 59, 60, 61
K.OA.A.5	Fluently add and subtract within 5.	62, 63, 64, 65, 66, 67, 68

Kindergarten Common Core State Standards for Mathematical Content

K.NBT   Number and Operations in Base Ten

St. #	Standard	Pages in This Book that Support the Standard
Work with numbers 11-19 to gain foundations for place value.		
K.NBT.A.1	Compose and decompose numbers from 11 to 19 into ten ones and some further ones, e.g., by using objects or drawings, and record each composition or decomposition by a drawing or equation (such as 18 = 10 + 8); understand that these numbers are composed of ten ones and one, two, three, four, five, six, seven, eight, or nine ones.	70, 71, 72, 73, 74, 75, 75, 77, 78

K.MD   Measurement and Data

St. #	Standard	Pages in This Book that Support the Standard
Describe and compare measurable attributes.		
K.MD.A.1	Describe measurable attributes of objects, such as length or weight. Describe several measurable attributes of a single object.	80, 81, 82, 83, 84, 85, 86, 87, 88
K.MD.A.2	Directly compare two objects with a measurable attribute in common, to see which object has "more of"/"less of" the attribute, and describe the difference. For example, directly compare the heights of two children and describe one child as taller/shorter.	83, 84, 85, 86, 87, 88
Classify objects and count the number of objects in each category.		
K.MD.B.3	Classify objects into given categories; count the numbers of objects in each category and sort the categories by count.	85, 86, 87, 88

Kindergarten Common Core State Standards for Mathematical Content

K.G   Geometry

St. #	Standard	Pages in This Book that Support the Standard
Identify and describe shapes.		
K.G.A.1	Describe objects in the environment using names of shapes, and describe the relative positions of these objects using terms such as *above, below, beside, in front of, behind,* and *next to.*	108-109, 110, 111, 112-113, 114, 115
K.G.A.2	Compose two-dimensional shapes (rectangles, squares, trapezoids, triangles, half-circles, and quarter-circles) or three-dimensional shapes (cubes, right rectangular prisms, right circular cones, and right circular cylinders) to create a composite shape, and compose new shapes from the composite shape.	116-117, 118-119, 120-121
K.G.A.3	Partition circles and rectangles into two and four equal shares, describe the shares using the words *halves, fourths,* and *quarters,* and use the phrases *half of, fourth of,* and *quarter of.* Describe the whole as *two of,* or *four of,* the shares. Understand for these examples that decomposing into more equal shares creates smaller shares.	121-122, 125-126
Analyze, compare, create, and compose shapes.		
K.G.B.4	Analyze and compare two- and three-dimensional shapes, in different sizes and orientations, using informal language to describe their similarities, differences, parts (e.g., number of sides and vertices/"corners") and other attributes (e.g., having sides of equal length).	95, 99, 100, 101, 102
K.G.B.5	Model shapes in the world by building shapes from components (e.g., sticks and clay balls) and drawing shapes.	103, 104, 105, 106
K.G.B.6	Compose simple shapes to form larger shapes. For example, *"Can you join these two triangles with full sides touching to make a rectangle?"*	104, 105, 106

COUNTING AND CARDINALITY

Kindergarten

One Little, Two Little

Learn this dinosaur verse. Chant it, sing it, and act it out.

One little, **two** little, **three** little dinosaurs

Four little, **five** little, **six** little dinosaurs

Seven little, **eight** little, **nine** little dinosaurs

Ten little dinosaurs standing end to end

Ten little, **nine** little, **eight** little dinosaurs

Seven little, **six** little, **five** little dinosaurs

Four little, **three** little, **two** little dinosaurs

One little dinosaur looking for a friend

Name

Move Like a Dinosaur

Think about the dinosaurs as you count.

Walk like an enormous T-rex.
Count to **20** steps.

Tyrannosaurus rex was a huge, fierce dinosaur that was about 40 feet (12 meters) long. It could rear up to a height of 18 feet (5.5 meters).

Walk like a tiny Wannanosaurus.
Count to **20** steps.

Wannanosaurus was a tiny herbivorous, or plant eating, dinosaur weighing about ten pounds (4.5 kilograms), and standing about 3 feet (1 meter) tall.

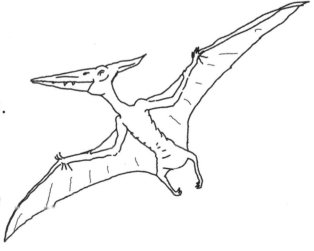

Pteranodon, wave your giant wings.
Flap **20** times.

Pteranodon, a flying reptile, flew through the air with wings that were up to 39 feet (12 meters) from tip to tip.

Name

Count by Ones and Tens
Common Core Reinforcement Activities — Kindergarten Math

How Far Can You Count?

Practice counting aloud.

Just count by ones. How far can you count?

1... 2... 3...

For each step the T-rex takes, the Wannanosaurus will need to take **ten** steps. Count by **ten.** How far can you count?

Name

Count the Bones

Some children visit a museum to see dinosaur skeletons.
Imagine the bones as you help the children count.

Sam likes to count the plates on the back of the Stegosaurus. He has already counted **7** plates. Count on. Start with **8**. Stop when you get to **20**.

Tam counts the rib bones on the Ankylosaurus skeleton. She has already counted **9**.
Keep counting for her. Stop when you get to **15**.

Pam counts the bones in the dinosaur's tail. She has counted **12**. Keep counting. Stop when you get to **20**.

Name

Count Forward from a Given Number
Common Core Reinforcement Activities — Kindergarten Math

Counting On with Big Numbers

Counting aloud is fun! Help HeeJee, Missy, and Ethan count.

HeeJee is counting the teeth on one side of a duck-billed dinosaur's jaw. He has counted to **23**. Count on. Stop when you get to **50**.

Duck-billed dinosaurs had plates of big grinding teeth on each side of their jaws. There were sometimes 2,000 teeth on one plate.

Missy is counting the pages in her dinosaur book. She has counted **30**. Keep counting for her. Stop when you get to **60**.

Ethan counts the spikes on the Gastonia. He has counted **17**. Keep counting. Stop when you get to **45**.

Gastonia, one of the first Ankylosaurs, or armored dinosaurs, had short legs and rows of spikes covering its head, shoulders, back, and tail.

Name

What Number Is Next?

Listen as someone reads the number on each dinosaur's tail.

Tell what number would come next if you were counting on.

Name

Count Forward from a Given Number
Common Core Reinforcement Activities — Kindergarten Math

And the Next Number Is...

Listen as someone reads the number on each dinosaur's sign. Tell what number would come next if you were counting on.

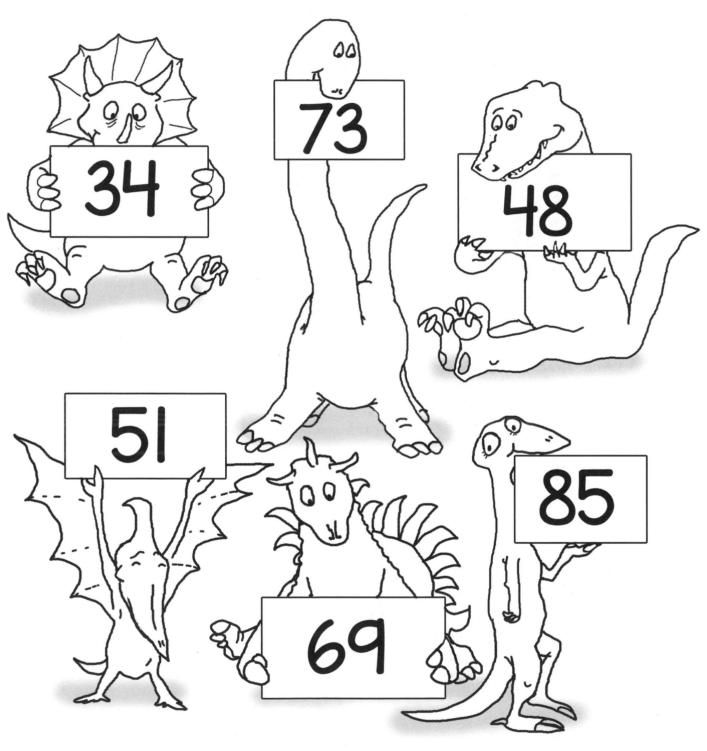

Name

Write and Draw

Practice writing the numbers.
Trace each one.
Then write two of your own.

1 ___ ___

2 ___ ___

3 ___ ___

4 ___ ___

5 ___ ___

| Draw one thing. |
| Draw two things. |
| Draw three things. |
| Draw four things. |
| Draw five things. |

Name

Write Numbers 0 to 5
Common Core Reinforcement Activities — Kindergarten Math

What's Under the Rock?

Materials: *Dinosaur Counters (page 108); Dinosaur Number Cards 0-5 (pages 112-113); child-safe scissors*

To the teacher: Give each pair of students the "paper rock" portion of this page, a scissors to cut out the rock, and five dinosaur counters. Place the 6 number cards (0, 1, 2, 3, 4, 5) between the students. Read the rest of the directions to the students.

Play this game with a partner. Your partner looks away. You choose a card. Take that number of counters. Arrange them and cover them with the paper rock. Give your partner a flash peek under the rock. Your partner names the number. Take turns hiding and showing the counters.

Name

Flash and Tell

Materials: *child-safe scissors*

Play this game as partners. Cut out the cards. One partner flashes a card for five seconds. The other partner tells how many dinosaurs were on the card.

Names

Perceive Number without Counting
Common Core Reinforcement Activities — Kindergarten Math

Counting Dinosaurs

Materials: *ten Dinosaur Counters for each student (page 108); Number Lines (page 111)*

Grab some dinosaur counters. Put one counter under each number on your number line paper. In the first row below, color the number of squares to show how many dinosaurs you counted. Repeat this seven more times. Each time, color squares to show the number you took.

GRAB #1	1	2	3	4	5	6	7	8	9	10
GRAB #2	1	2	3	4	5	6	7	8	9	10
GRAB #3	1	2	3	4	5	6	7	8	9	10
GRAB #4	1	2	3	4	5	6	7	8	9	10
GRAB #5	1	2	3	4	5	6	7	8	9	10
GRAB #6	1	2	3	4	5	6	7	8	9	10
GRAB #7	1	2	3	4	5	6	7	8	9	10
GRAB #8	1	2	3	4	5	6	7	8	9	10

Name

Race to Trace

Materials: *one number cube (die) for each pair of students*

Play with a partner. One should sit on each side of the paper. Take turns rolling a number cube. Trace the number on this record sheet that matches the number of dots on the cube. Keep going until one player has traced all of the numbers on the sheet. If a number comes up after you've traced it twice, skip your turn.

Name

Name

Pair One Object with One Number
Common Core Reinforcement Activities — Kindergarten Math

How Many Dinos?

Write a numeral to tell how many dinosaurs you see.

1 | 2

3 | 4

Name

Count the Nest

Write a numeral to tell how many you see in the big picture.

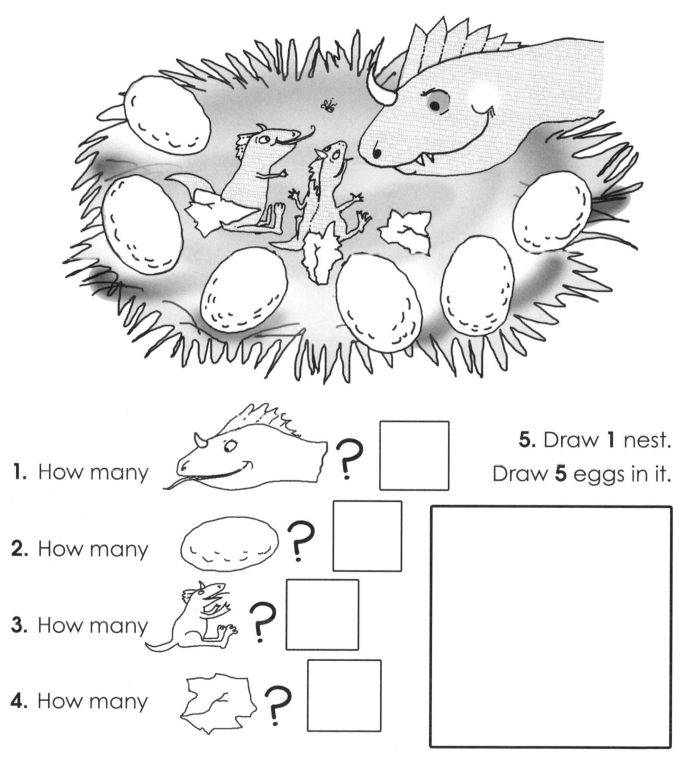

1. How many ❓ ☐

2. How many ❓ ☐

3. How many ❓ ☐

4. How many ❓ ☐

5. Draw **1** nest.
Draw **5** eggs in it.

Name

Pair One Object with One Number
Common Core Reinforcement Activities — Kindergarten Math

Match the Pattern

Materials: *Footprint Counters (page 109)*

For each section, use counters to make a pattern that matches the pattern of footprints. Arrange your counters next to your paper. Write a number in the box to tell how many.

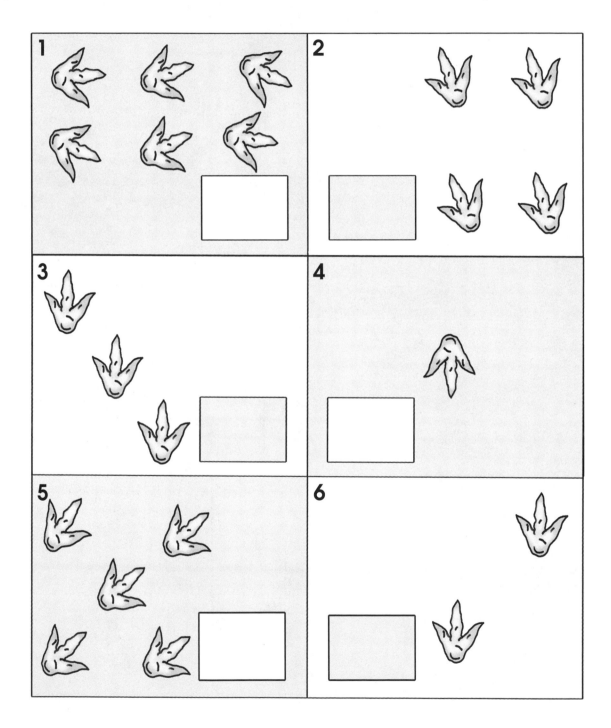

Name

Grab and Count

Materials: *container of 100 Fossil Counters for each group of 3-4 students*
(page 110)

Play with two friends. Take turns. Grab a handful of counters.
Count how many. Then write the number in your column.
Repeat this until you fill each space on this record sheet.

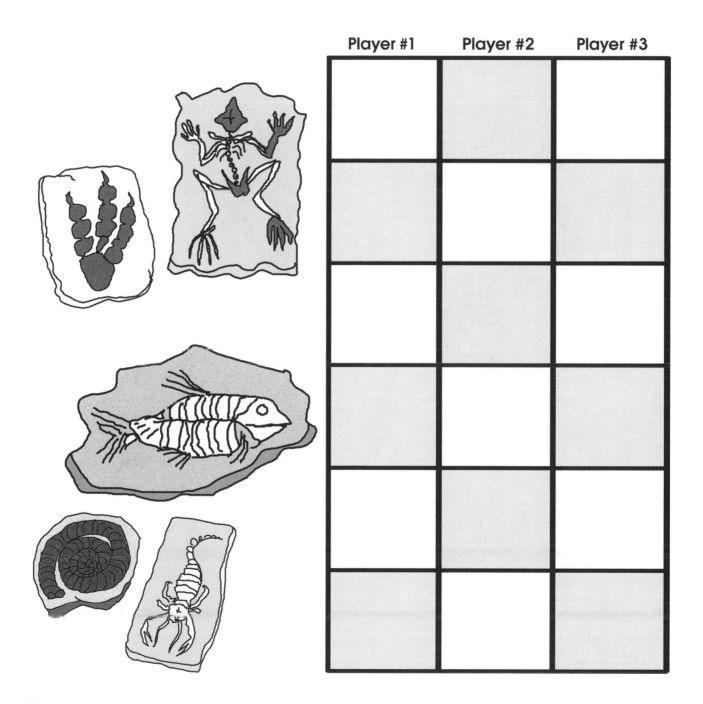

Player #1	Player #2	Player #3

Names

Pair One Object with One Number
Common Core Reinforcement Activities — Kindergarten Math

Count the Triceratops

Point and touch to count the different parts of the Triceratops.

1. How many eyes does it have? _____

2. How many legs does it have? _____

3. How many tails does it have? _____

4. What else can you
count on the Triceratops?

5. Color the Triceratops yellow. Color the polka dots purple.

Name

Count the Bonehead

This is a boneheaded dinosaur called the Stygimoloch.

Point and touch to count the different parts of the Stygimoloch.

1. How many horns does it have? _____

2. How many toes does it have on one foot? _____

3. How many fingers does it have on one hand? _____

4. What else can you count on the Stygimoloch?

_____

5. Draw five stripes on the dinosaur's back.

Name

Connect Counting to Cardinality
Common Core Reinforcement Activities — Kindergarten Math

Count the Stegosaurus

Point and touch to count the Stegosaurus.

1. How many plates does it have on its back? _____

2. How many legs does it have? _____

3. How many spikes does it have
on the very end of its tail? _____

4. How many eyes does it have? _____

5. Draw your own dinosaur on the back of this page
and invite someone to count its different parts.

Name

Count and Ask

Materials: *20 or more Dinosaur Counters for each pair of students (page 108)*

Read a challenge. Count out the dinosaurs. Ask your partner, "How many are there?" If your partner answers correctly, check off the challenge and move to the next. Take turns counting and asking the question.

Challenges:

Lay the counters here as you count.

- [ ] Count out **8** dinosaurs.

- [ ] Count out **15** dinosaurs.

- [ ] Count out **6** dinosaurs.

- [ ] Count out **19** dinosaurs.

- [ ] Count out **7** dinosaurs.

- [ ] Count out **13** dinosaurs.

- [ ] Count out **20** dinosaurs.

- [ ] Count out **9** dinosaurs.

Names

Count to Answer "How many?"
Common Core Reinforcement Activities — Kindergarten Math

Compare the Counters

Materials: *number cubes (two per student pair); Dinosaur Counters (page 108)*

Play with a partner. Roll two number cubes. Count the dots. Build a set of counters to match the number of dots. Keep this set while your partner rolls and builds a set. Compare your sets. Circle the word that tells how your number compares to your partner's.

Turn 1: I have _____ counters.

My partner has _____.

My number is: more.

          less.

          the same.

Turn 3: I have _____ counters.

My partner has _____.

My number is: more.

          less.

          the same.

Turn 2: I have _____ counters.

My partner has _____.

My number is: more.

          less.

          the same.

Turn 4: I have _____ counters.

My partner has _____.

My number is: more.

          less.

          the same.

Turn 5: I have _____ counters.

My partner has _____.

My number is: more.

          less.

          the same.

Names

Dinosaurs in the Lakes

Materials: *number cube for each pair, Dinosaur Counters (page 108);*
Swamp Mats (page 115)

Take turns with a partner. Roll a number cube. Put that number of dinosaur counters in one lake on your swamp mat. Roll again. Put that number of counters in the second lake. Use this page to record the numbers of dinosaurs in the lakes. Compare the two numbers. Use blue to color the lake with the greater number. Repeat this for five turns.

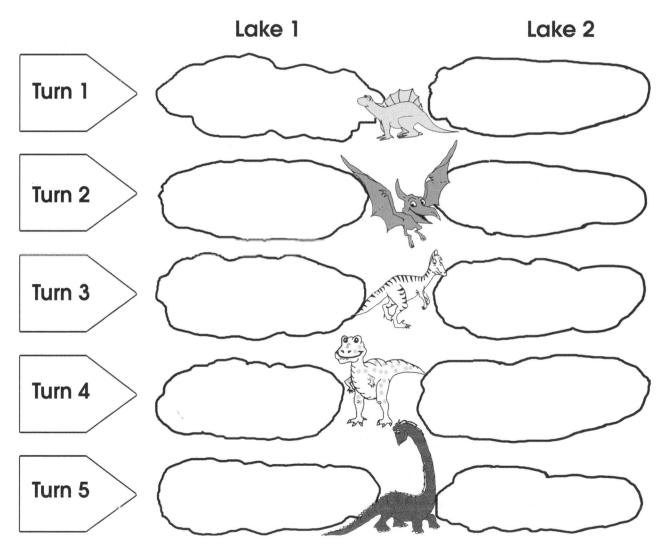

	Lake 1	Lake 2
Turn 1		
Turn 2		
Turn 3		
Turn 4		
Turn 5		

Was there a time when one group was not more? Why?

Names

Compare Written Numbers 1 to 10
Common Core Reinforcement Activities — Kindergarten Math

Prove It!

Materials: *Have available: Dinosaur Counters (page 108); Footprint Counters (109); Fossil Counters (page 110)*

Circle the number in each pair below that is more.
Explain how you could prove it.

A. 8   6

B. 4   7

C. 3   1

D. 9   6

E. 2   8

F. 5   4

G. 9   5

H. 7   3

I. 7   9

J. 0   10

Name

Number Battle

Materials: *two sets of Dinosaur Number Cards 0-10 (pages 112-114)*
for each pair

To the teacher:

1. Group students in pairs. Shuffle two sets of cards together for each pair.

2. When directed, each player will draw two cards from the top of the deck.

3. Students will examine the cards and orally report their numbers.

Player 1: "I have _____ and _____."   Player 2: "I have _____ and _____."

4. Then, using those four numbers, the players work together to complete one or more sentence frames on the record sheet. (See page 42.) The sentence frames look like this: _____ is greater than _____

For example, if a pair draws 2, 5, 5, and 8, they may write:

"8 is greater than 5" and "5 is greater than 2."

5. Each card from a draw may be used only once, so players should act strategically to arrange cards to get the most correct statements as possible.

6. Students shuffle and reuse cards to complete a total of 10 sentence frames. This may take 10 draws or fewer. Challenge students to keep working at this until they can do it in five draws.

7. Give each pair of students a record sheet (page 42). Explain the following:

Each of you draw two cards. Report your numbers out loud like this:

"I have _____ **and** _____."

Next, compare your four numbers. Finish one or more sentence frames. Use each number only once. Then shuffle the cards and draw again. Keep doing this until you finish 10 sentence frames.

Use with page 42.

Compare Written Numbers 1 to 10
Common Core Reinforcement Activities — Kindergarten Math

Number Battle, continued

Number Battle Sentence Frames

1. _____ is greater than _____.

2. _____ is greater than _____.

3. _____ is greater than _____.

4. _____ is greater than _____.

5. _____ is greater than _____.

6. _____ is greater than _____.

7. _____ is greater than _____.

8. _____ is greater than _____.

9. _____ is greater than _____.

10. _____ is greater than _____.

We took_____turns.

Can you do all 10 frames in fewer turns?

Use with page 41.

Name

OPERATIONS AND ALGEBRAIC THINKING

Kindergarten

Tell a Story

Look at the picture. Tell a math story about the dinosaurs in the story. Tell the same story in a different way with objects, drawings, or numbers.

Name

Act It Out

Work in groups of four. Look at the picture. Act out a math story about the dinosaurs in the story. Be ready to tell the math story in words and in numbers.

Names

Addition and Subtraction Processes
Common Core Reinforcement Activities — Kindergarten Math

Clap and Stomp a Problem

Follow the picture prompts to clap and stomp.

 tells you to clap.

 tells you to stomp.

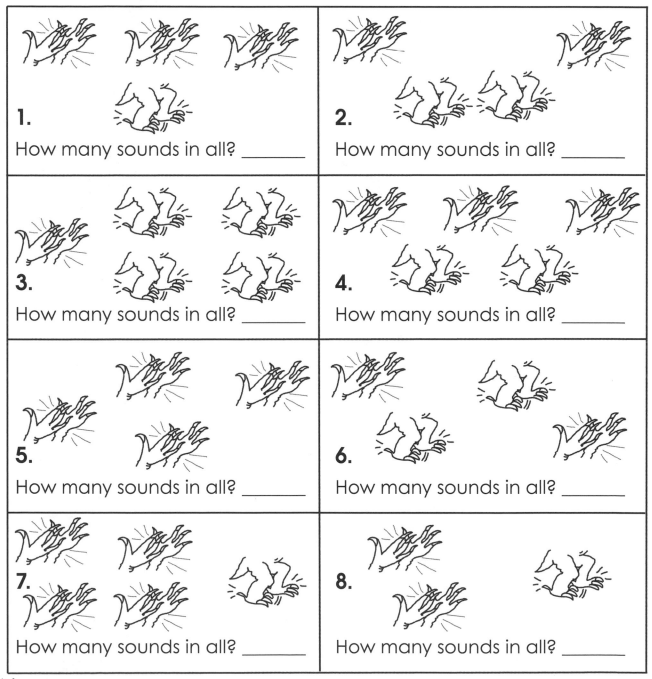

1. How many sounds in all? _____

2. How many sounds in all? _____

3. How many sounds in all? _____

4. How many sounds in all? _____

5. How many sounds in all? _____

6. How many sounds in all? _____

7. How many sounds in all? _____

8. How many sounds in all? _____

Name

Draw a Story

Draw a math story with dinosaurs.

Be ready to tell the story to a friend.

Name

Addition and Subtraction Processes
Common Core Reinforcement Activities — Kindergarten Math

Story Show and Tell

Materials: *all ten Dinosaur Cutouts (pages 116-117)*

Think about a math story. Draw the story in the boxes to show each step. Use the cutouts as puppets to tell the story.

First

Then

Finally

Name

Math Comes Alive!

Materials: *Swamp Mat (page 115) and five Dinosaur Cutouts (page 116)*

Use the dinosaur cutouts to make these math stories come to life.

1

2 dinosaurs were standing in the water. **1** more dinosaur came. How many dinosaurs are there now?

2

1 dinosaur was by the tree. **1** more dinosaur came. How many dinosaurs are there now?

Make up a new math story and show it with the dinosaurs. Then draw or write it in the frame below.

3

Name

Addition Word Problems
Common Core Reinforcement Activities — Kindergarten Math

Dinosaurs in the Swamp

Materials: *Swamp Mat (page 115) and five Dinosaur Cutouts (page 117)*

Use the dinosaurs to show the math stories.
Retell the stories to a friend.

1. The swamp was empty.
Four dinosaurs came.
How many dinosaurs are
there in all?

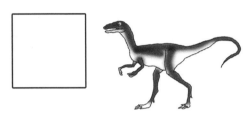

2. Three dinosaurs
munched on leaves. One
more dinosaur stopped for
lunch. How many dinosaurs
are there in all?

3. One dinosaur stopped to
rest by the water. Two more
dinosaurs stopped to rest.
How many dinosaurs are
there in all?

4. Two dinosaurs stood in
the water. Three dinosaurs
waded in with them. How
many dinosaurs are there
in all?

Name

How Many Babies?

The dinosaur eggs are hatching. Read and solve the story problems about the hatching babies.

1. One egg cracked and the baby dinosaur came out of its shell. Seven more hatched. How many dinosaur babies are there in the nest?

2. Four baby dinosaurs poked their heads out of the broken shells. Three more popped out. How many dinosaur babies are there in the nest?

3. Six baby dinosaurs crawled around in the nest. The last egg didn't hatch. How many dinosaur babies hatched in all?

4. A nest has four babies on the left side and four babies on the right side. How many babies are in the nest?

Name

Addition Word Problems
Common Core Reinforcement Activities — Kindergarten Math

Count and Subtract

Materials: *Swamp Mat (page 115) and five Dinosaur Cutouts (page 116 or 117)*

Cut out the dinosaurs.

Use them to make these math stories come to life.

1

Three dinosaurs were standing in the water. One dinosaur plodded home. How many dinosaurs are there now?

2

Four dinosaurs were looking for food. Two found some tasty leaves high above. How many dinosaurs are still hungry?

Make up a new math story and show it with the dinosaurs. Then draw or write it in the frame below.

3

Name

Losing Dinosaurs

Alexander loved his toy dinosaurs, but he was always losing them. Read and solve the story problems about the lost toys.

1. Alexander put **7** dinosaurs on the bed. His little sister jumped on the bed and knocked **2** off. How many dinosaurs are still on the bed?

2. Alexander carried **10** dinosaurs in his pocket to keep them safe. When he was hanging upside down on the bars, **4** dinosaurs fell out. How many dinosaurs are still safe?

3. Alexander had **8** Apatosaurus toys. He broke the neck on **1** of the dinosaurs and had to throw it away. How many does he have now?

4. Alexander put all **5** of his dinosaurs in a safe place, but he forgot where he put them. How many of his dinosaurs are now in his hand?

5. Alexander loves his **9** T-rex toys. His dog chewed **3** of them to bits. How many whole T-rexes does Alexander have now?

Name

Subtraction Word Problems
Common Core Reinforcement Activities — Kindergarten Math

Hiding in the Swamp

The dinosaurs are playing a game of hide and seek.

Read the problems and draw pictures to solve them.

1. **4** dinosaurs were hiding in the trees.
   1 was a Stegosaurus. How many
   were not Stegosauruses?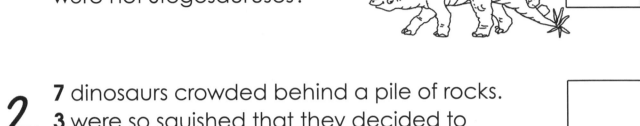

2. **7** dinosaurs crowded behind a pile of rocks.
   3 were so squished that they decided to
   find a new hiding spot. How many stayed
   behind the rocks?

3. **8** tiny Wannasauruses huddled beside a log.
   2 of them decided to crawl into the log.
   How many are left outside?

4. **6** dinosaurs hid behind a giant fern. **1** of
   the dinosaurs was so hungry that it ate all
   the leaves off the branches around it so it
   wasn't hidden any more. How many are still
   out of sight?

5. **3** dinosaurs hid inside a dark cave.
   2 were so scared that they ran out.
   How many dinosaurs are left in
   the cave?

Name _____

Add or Subtract?

Read the problem. Think about whether you will add to solve the problem or whether you will subtract. Circle your choice. Draw a picture in the box to find the answer.

1. Oviraptor is looking for food. She sees **3** young plant-eaters plodding to the water. If Oviraptor catches **1**, how many will be left?

   I will add.
   I will subtract.

2. Diplodocus is looking for some leaves to eat. He sees a branch with **6** leaves on one side and **4** leaves on the other side. How many leaves are on the branch?

   I will add.
   I will subtract.

3. Pteranodon flies high over the trees. He sees **1** T-rex, **2** Duckbills, and **3** Triceratops. How many dinosaurs does he see?

   I will add.
   I will subtract.

4. **7** Iguanodons rested near the trees. **3** ran to the lake for a swim. How many are still resting?

   I will add.
   I will subtract.

Name

Addition and Subtraction Word Problems
Common Core Reinforcement Activities — Kindergarten Math

Draw and Explain

Draw a picture to solve each problem.

Tell about your thinking.

1

Four dinosaurs get stuck in the mud. Two of them are duck-billed dinosaurs. The others are Iguanodons. How many Iguanodons are there?

Change the story. What if three of them are duck-billed dinosaurs? How many Iguanodons are there?

2

Five dinosaurs are eating leaves. Three of them have long necks. How many have short necks?

Change the story. Pretend four of them have long necks. How many have short necks?

Name

Change the Story

Materials: *ten Dinosaur Cutouts (pages 116, 117)*

Use dinosaur cutouts to tell the stories and solve the problems.

See two examples below.

1. Seven dinosaurs hunt for food. Four of them like plants. The rest like meat. How many like meat?

   Change the story. Pretend there are five plant eaters. How many are meat eaters?

2. Six dinosaurs have spikes. Two of them have spikes on their tails but not on their backs. The rest have spikes on their backs but not on their tails. How many have spikes on their backs?

   Change the story. Pretend there are three with spiked tails. How many have spiked backs?

3. A herd of nine dinosaurs explore the swamp. Three are adults. How many are children?

   Change the story. Pretend seven are adults. How many are children?

Name

Decompose Numbers
Common Core Reinforcement Activities — Kindergarten Math

Start with Ten

Draw two story problems that begin with **ten** toy dinosaurs in Sophie's pocket. Tell the problems to a friend and ask your friend to solve them.

1

2

Name

Making Ten

Materials: *Fossil Counters (page 110) reproduced on red and yellow paper*

Use counters. Make sets of ten.

1. Start with **8** red counters. Add yellow counters to make **10** in all. Draw to show what you did.

2. Start with **2** red counters. Add yellow counters to make **10** in all. Draw to show what you did.

3. Start with **6** red counters. Add yellow counters to make **10** in all. Draw to show what you did.

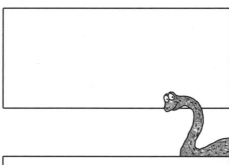

4. Start with **1** red counter. Add yellow counters to make **10** in all. Draw to show what you did.

5. Start with **3** red counters. Add yellow counters to make **10** in all. Draw to show what you did.

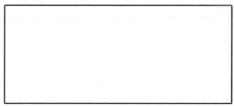

6. Start with **5** red counters. Add yellow counters to make **10** in all. Draw to show what you did.

Name

Pair Numbers that Make Ten
Common Core Reinforcement Activities — Kindergarten Math

Ten Turtle Eggs Total

Turtles lived at the same time as dinosaurs and still live today. Draw more turtle eggs in each row to make ten in all. Write the number in the box that tells how many you drew.

1 3 turtle eggs + [ ] turtle eggs = 10 eggs

2 9 turtle eggs + [ ] turtle eggs = 10 eggs

3 5 turtle eggs + [ ] turtle eggs = 10 eggs

4 2 turtle eggs + [ ] turtle eggs = 10 eggs

5 7 turtle eggs + [ ] turtle eggs = 10 eggs

6 4 turtle eggs + [ ] turtle eggs = 10 eggs

Name

Pair Numbers that Make Ten
Common Core Reinforcement Activities — Kindergarten Math

Hide-and-Seek Dinosaurs

Materials: *paper "rock" (pattern on page 26); Dinosaur Counters (page 108); child-safe scissors*

Play this game in pairs. Cut out a paper rock. Count out and arrange 10 dinosaurs. Close your eyes while your partner covers part of the set with the paper rock. Open your eyes and tell how many are covered. Take turns with your partner.

1. I see _____ so _____ are covered. _____ + _____ = 10

2. I see _____ so _____ are covered. _____ + _____ = 10

3. I see _____ so _____ are covered. _____ +_____ = 10

4. I see _____ so _____ are covered. _____ + _____ = 10

5. I see _____ so _____ are covered. _____ + _____ = 10

6. I see _____ so_____ are covered. _____ + _____ = 10

7. I see _____ so _____ are covered. _____ + _____ = 10

8. I see _____ so _____ are covered. _____ + _____ = 10

Names

Pair Numbers that Make Ten
Common Core Reinforcement Activities — Kindergarten Math

Race to Five

Materials: *Dinosaur Number Cards 0 to 5, six of each numeral (pages 112, 113); three each of two different counters (pages 108-110); number lines (below) for each student*

To the teacher: Explain and demonstrate Game 1. Play this before introducing Game 2. Students play the games in pairs, beginning with shuffled cards face down.

Game 1 Directions:

1. Each player starts with a counter on the zero on each number line.

2. One player flips a card to reveal a number and moves that many spaces across any one of his or her number lines. The second player takes a turn.

3. Play continues with players taking turns. The goal is to get all three counters to five on a number line before the other player. If a player is unable to move the number of spaces indicated on the card, the turn is forfeited.

Game 2 Directions:

Play the game in the same way as Game 1, but allow players to decompose a number into smaller numbers to be used on multiple number lines. For example: if player has a counter on three and picks four, she or he can move the first counter forward two spaces to make five and then move another counter two spaces.

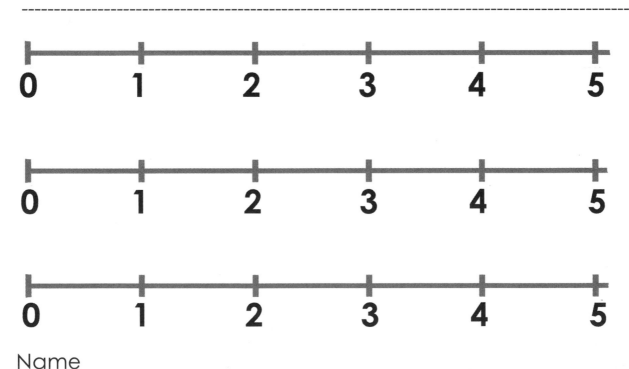

Hunt a Dinosaur!

Materials: *Dinosaur Number Cards 0 to 5, six of each numeral (pages 112, 113); Dinosaur Habitat for each player (page 118); record sheet for each student (below)*

To the teacher: This game requires students to find pairs of cards that equal five. Students play the games in pairs, beginning with shuffled cards face down.

1. Each player draws three cards and places them face up behind the folded dinosaur habitat paper (screen). Players combine any two cards to make five, if they can. They place cards beside the screen.

2. Taking turns, one player asks the other for a card that can be combined with his or her card to make five. For example: If Brie has a three card, she asks, "Do you have a two?" If the partner does, he or she gives it to Brie and Brie displays the pair beside the screen. If not, the partner says: "Hunt a dinosaur!" and Brie must draw a dinosaur card from the stack. The first player to move all of his or her hidden dinosaur cards to pairs of cards equaling five wins the game. Students can record their actions on the record below.

My Record—Hunt a Dinosaur!

I made these pairs.

☐ + ☐ = 5   ☐ + ☐ = 5

☐ + ☐ = 5   ☐ + ☐ = 5

☐ + ☐ = 5   ☐ + ☐ = 5

Name _____

Fluently Add and Subtract within Five
Common Core Reinforcement Activities — Kindergarten Math

Use Your Head

Solve the problems quickly in your head. Then cut out the small crocodiles and use them with the five-frame to check the problem.

1. 0 + 5 = _____   **3.** 2 + 3 = _____   **5.** 4 + 1 = _____

2. 1 + 4 = _____   **4.** 3 + 2 = _____   **6.** 5 + 0 = _____

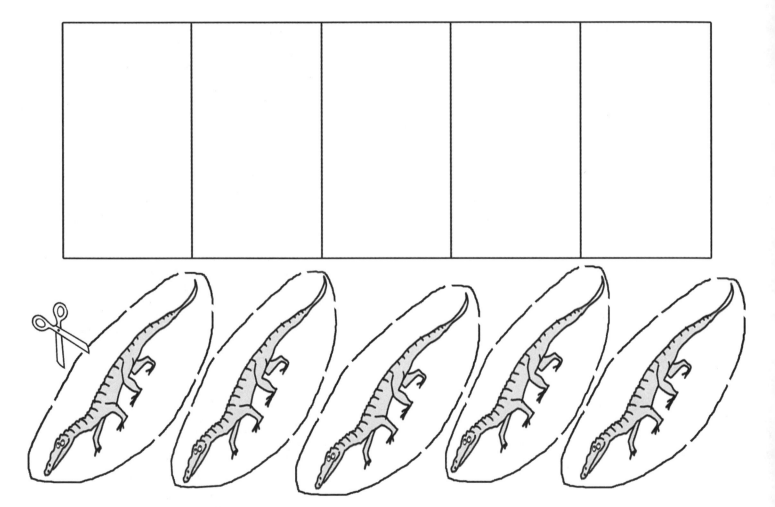

The first crocodiles lived around the same time as many dinosaurs. Several types of crocodiles live in parts of the world today.

Name _____

Mental Math

Solve the problems quickly in your head. Then cut out the turtle pictures and use them with the five-frame to check the problem.

1. 5 - 0 = _____ **3.** 5 - 1 = _____ **5.** 5 - 2 = _____

2. 5 - 3 = _____ **4.** 5 - 4 = _____ **6.** 5 - 5 = _____

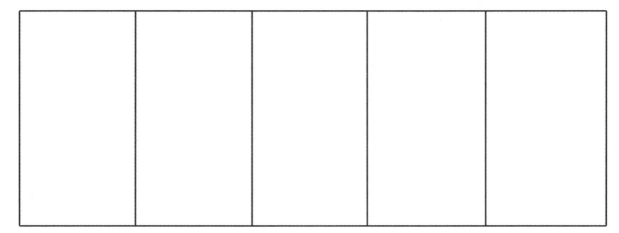

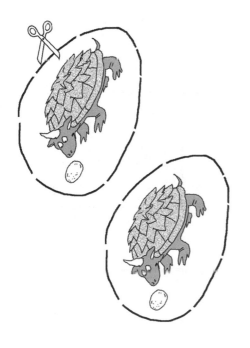

Name

Fluently Add and Subtract within Five
Common Core Reinforcement Activities — Kindergarten Math

How Will You Solve It?

Materials: *Footprint Counters (page 109)*

Read each problem. Think about what is missing from each problem. Think about how you will solve each problem.

Solve each problem. Tell a friend how you did it.

Use the five-frame and the footprint counters to show your thinking.

1. $2 + \boxed{} = 4$

2. $1 + \boxed{} = 3$

3. $4 + \boxed{} = 5$

4. $0 + \boxed{} = 2$

5. $3 + \boxed{} = 5$

6. $5 + \boxed{} = 5$

Name

How Will You Find It?

Materials: *Fossil Counters (page 110)*

Read each problem. Think about the missing number for each problem and how you will find it.

Solve each problem. Tell a friend how you did it.

Use the five-frame and the fossil counters to show your thinking.

1. 2 + ☐ = 4   **5.** 0 + ☐ = 2

2. 1 + ☐ = 3   **6.** 3 + ☐ = 5

3. 4 + ☐ = 5   **7.** 5 + ☐ = 5

4. 3 + ☐ = 5   **8.** 4 + ☐ = 4

Name

Fluently Add and Subtract within Five
Common Core Reinforcement Activities — Kindergarten Math

Four Problems, One Answer

Make up four problems that all have the answer 5.

Draw or write each problem in a separate box.

Share your problems with a friend. Listen to your friend's problems, too. Were any the same?

Name

NUMBER AND OPERATIONS IN BASE TEN

Kindergarten

More Than Ten Dinosaurs

To the teacher: You may want to create a giant ten-frame in the middle of the students' gathering place and use students as counters to model this activity.

Write the number of dinosaurs in each problem.

1. How many Triceratops? _____

2. How many Triceratops? _____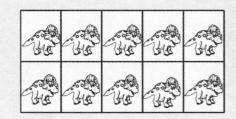

Is it easier to count the dinosaurs in #1 or #2? _____ Why?

3. How many 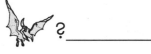?_____ Tell someone how you know.

4. How many ? _____

Tell someone how you know.

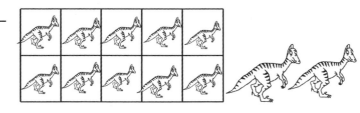

5. How many ? _____

Tell someone how you know.

Building the Teen Numbers

Materials: *counters (pages 108-110); Ten-Frames (page 119); Teen Number Cards (page 120)*

To the teacher: You may want to create a giant ten-frame in the middle of the students' gathering place and use paper plates as counters to model this activity. Demonstrate how to fill the frame from left to right, top to bottom, one counter per square. Model describing the final representation of the number: *We have ten ones on the ten-frame and ___ ones off the ten-frame.*

Place the cards number side down on a flat surface. Flip over a card. Use the ten-frame and some counters. Show the number by placing the counters on the ten-frame. Complete the sentence frame below for each card.

1. ___ is 10 on and ____ off.

2. ___ is 10 on and ____ off.

3. ___ is 10 on and ____ off.

4. ___ is 10 on and ____ off.

5. ___ is 10 on and ___ off.

6. ___ is 10 on and ___ off.

7. ___ is 10 on and ___ off.

8. ___ is 10 on and ____ off.

Name

Foundations for Place Value
Common Core Reinforcement Activities — Kindergarten Math

Building More Teen Numbers

Materials: *Dinosaur Counters (page 108); Ten-Frames (page 119); Teen Number Cards (page 120)*

Place the cards number side down on a flat surface. Flip over a card. Build the number by placing counters on the ten-frame. Explain what you did. Record your teen number in the square by the 1. Color in the small ten-frame to show your number. Use an X to show each extra dinosaur. Draw a new card and repeat the activity five more times.

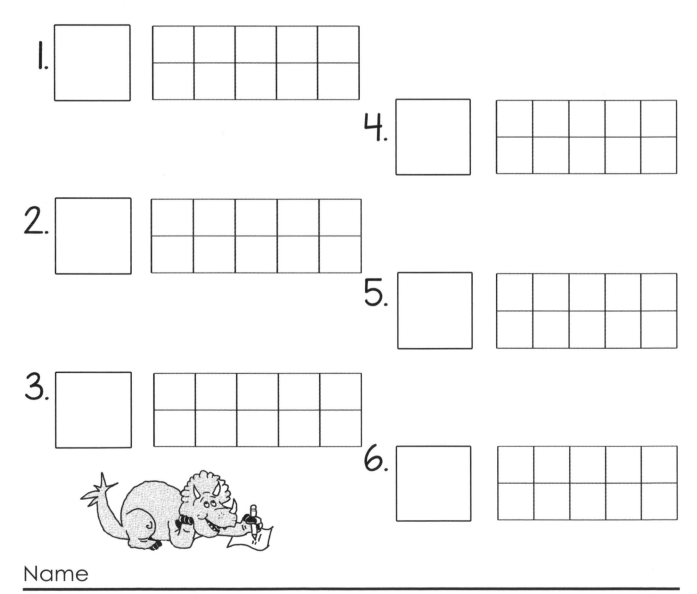

Name

Ten Ones in a Bunch

Materials: *straws or coffee stirring sticks; rubber bands; child-safe scissors; glue*

Here's a new way to show teen numbers. Instead of a ten-frame, bundle a group of ten straws or sticks to show ten ones. Use rubber bands to make bundles. Build each number. Then cut out the pictures below and glue them to a separate page to show what you did.

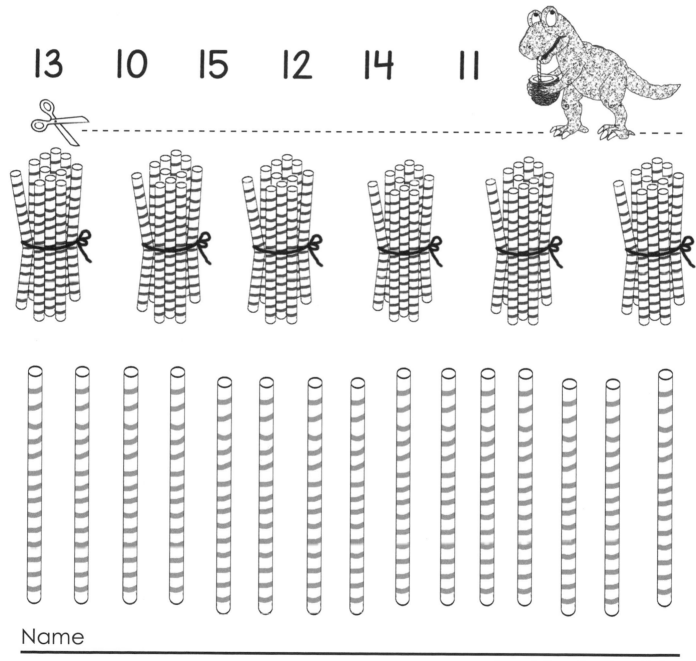

13   10   15   12   14   11

Name

Foundations for Place Value
Common Core Reinforcement Activities — Kindergarten Math

Ten Ones and More

Cut out the pictures below and glue them to a separate page to build each number.

16   18   17   20   19

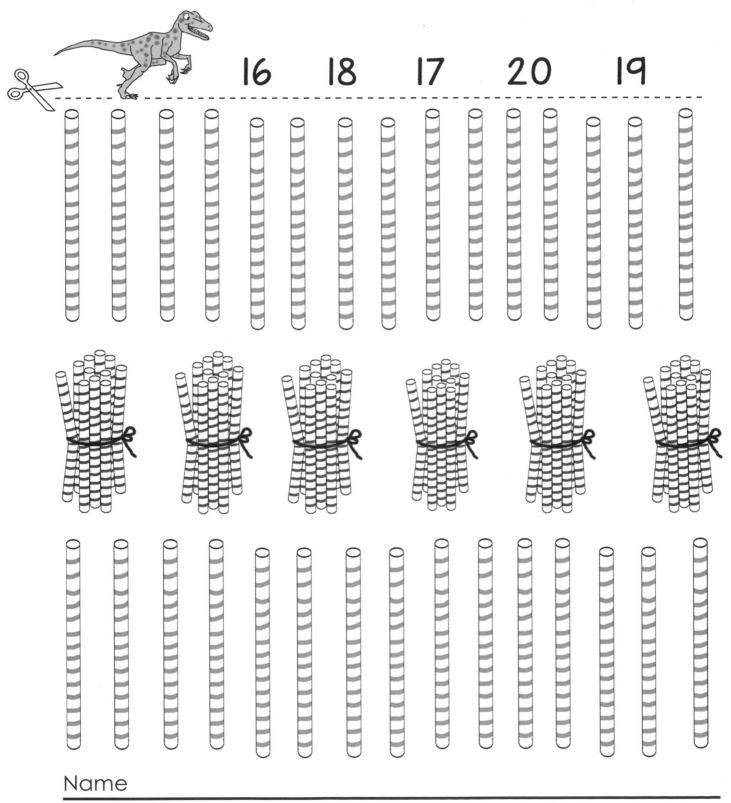

Boxes of Bones

Draw a line to match the numeral and the dinosaur bones.
There are ten bones in each box.

1. 12

2. 17

3. 14

4. 11

5. 15

6. 10

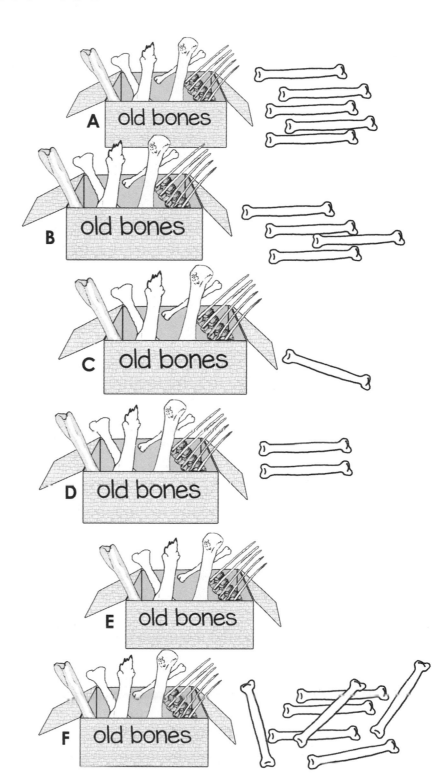

Name

Foundations for Place Value
Common Core Reinforcement Activities — Kindergarten Math

Sets of Ten Ones + a Few

Draw to show the tens and ones.

13	17
10	15
12	11
16	14

Name

Common Core Reinforcement Activities — Kindergarten Math

One Number Three Ways

The pictures show three ways to make 17.

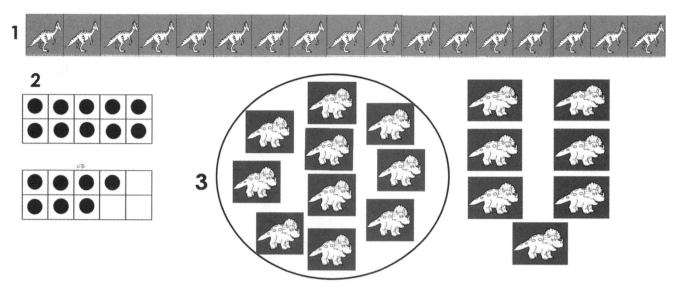

Show three ways to make each of these numbers. Use drawings or counters.

15

12

18

13

19

Name

Foundations for Place Value
Common Core Reinforcement Activities — Kindergarten Math

So Many Eggs!

Each nest has the same number of eggs. Draw any number (from 0 to 9) of extra eggs outside the nest. In the square, write a number to show the new total number of eggs.

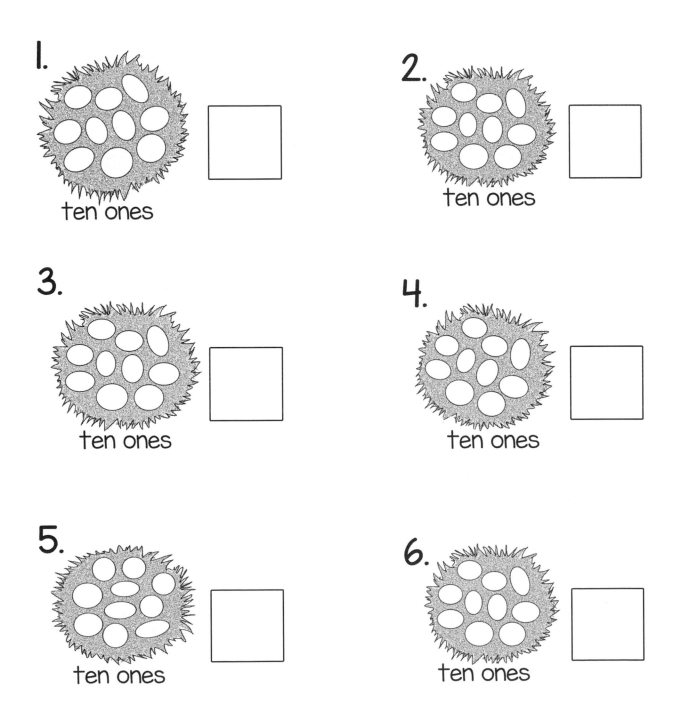

1. ten ones

2. ten ones

3. ten ones

4. ten ones

5. ten ones

6. ten ones

Name

MEASUREMENT AND DATA

Kindergarten

The Size of a Diplodocus

Talk about the dinosaur.

Is it big or small?

Is it long or short?

Do you think it is heavy or light?

How does it compare to the person?

The man is standing next to a Diplodocus skeleton.

Name

Measure It!

Materials: *connecting cubes or paper clips*

Measure the pictures of the dinosaur and the tree.
Use cubes or paper clips.

How long is the dinosaur? _____ units

How tall is the tree? _____ units

Talk about the weight of the dinosaur.

Name

Describe Measurable Attributes
Common Core Reinforcement Activities — Kindergarten Math

How Long Is the Bone?

Measure the bones. Use cubes or paper clips.

How long is each bone?

Talk about the size of the bones.

1.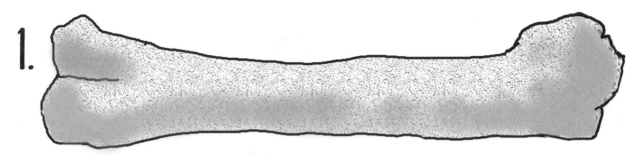

The bone is _____ units long.

2.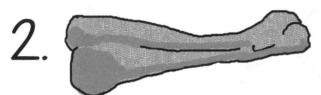

The bone is _____ units long.

3.

The bone is _____ units long.

4. The bone is _____ units long.

5.  The bone is _____ units long.

Name

Compare the Dinosaurs

Which dinosaur is taller? Which dinosaur is heavier?

Talk about the dinosaurs' tails.

Is one longer?

Is one spikier?

Do you think one would be
heavier than the other?

Name

Compare Measurable Attributes
Common Core Reinforcement Activities — Kindergarten Math

Alike and Different

Materials: *Dinosaurs for Sorting cards (pages 121-124)*

Choose two dinosaur cards. Look at the dinosaurs. Read about them. Think about how the dinosaurs are alike and how they are different. Explain your ideas.

Write to answer these questions.

1. Which one is taller? _____

2. Which one looks heavier? _____

3. Write one more way the dinosaurs are different.

The _____ is _____

than the _____ .

Name

Sorting Dinosaurs

Cut out the dinosaurs. Sort and glue them on the chart.

4-leg walkers	2-leg walkers

How many of these dinosaurs walked on two legs?

_____

Name

More Than One Way to Sort

Materials: *Dinosaurs for Sorting cards (pages 121-124)*

Choose one set of categories below. Cut out the labels and lay them on one chart. Sort the dinosaur cards into the categories. Show a friend. Pick a new pair of categories, cut out the new words, and sort the dinosaurs a different way.

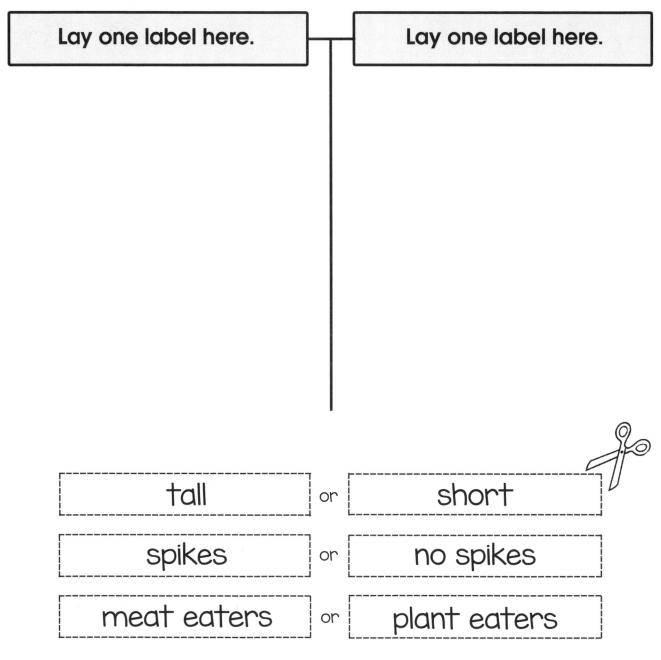

| Lay one label here. | Lay one label here. |

tall	or	short
spikes	or	no spikes
meat eaters	or	plant eaters

Name

A New Dinosaur

These three make-believe dinosaurs are all **Grinos.**

These three dinosaurs are **not** Grinos.

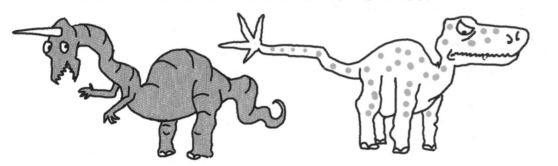

Think about the things that are the **same** about the Grinos and the things that make the other dinosaurs **different.**

Which of these is a **Grino?** (Circle it.)

A   B   C

Name

Sort Objects by Attribute
Common Core Reinforcement Activities — Kindergarten Math

Another New Dinosaur

These three make-believe dinosaurs are all **Coolosauruses.**

These three dinosaurs are not **Coolosauruses.**

Think about the things that are the **same** about the Coolosauruses and the things that make the other dinosaurs **different.** Which of these is a **Coolosaurus?** (Circle it.)

A   **B**   **C**

Name

GEOMETRY

Kindergarten

Where Is It?

Choose a dinosaur. Tell about how the dinosaur looks. Then tell about where it is.

Draw a line from the words to the correct dinosaur.

● behind
the tree

● above
the tree

● beside
the tree

● in front of
the tree

Name

Finish the Picture

The artist hasn't finished the picture. Finish drawing it for her.

Draw a dinosaur next to the rock.

Draw a tree beside the dinosaur.

Draw some grass under the rock.

Draw a sun above the tree.

Draw a turtle. Tell someone where it is.

Name

Use Position Words
Common Core Reinforcement Activities — Kindergarten Math

Find the Right Shape

Materials: *child-safe scissors; glue*

Cut around each dinosaur. Glue the correct dinosaur in each shape. Name the shape.

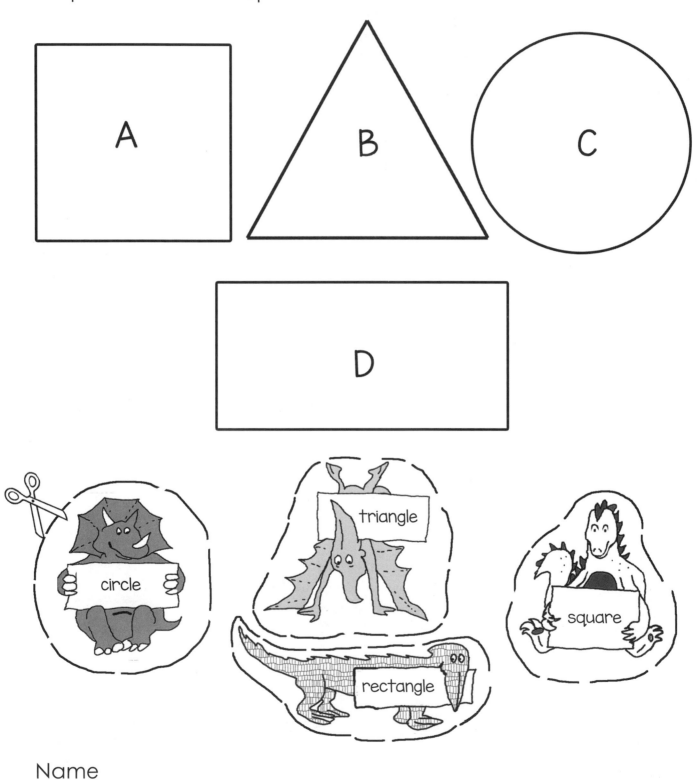

Sort and Tell

Materials: *Shapes for Sorting (page 126); child-safe scissors*

Start with the page titled "Shapes for Sorting." Cut out the shapes. Sort them. Tell someone about what you did.

circles

squares

rectangles

triangles

Name

Name Shapes
Common Core Reinforcement Activities — Kindergarten Math

How Many Sides?

Materials: *child-safe scissors; glue*

Count the sides of each shape. Cut around each dinosaur.
Glue the dinosaur in the correct shape to tell how many sides.
Can you name the shapes?

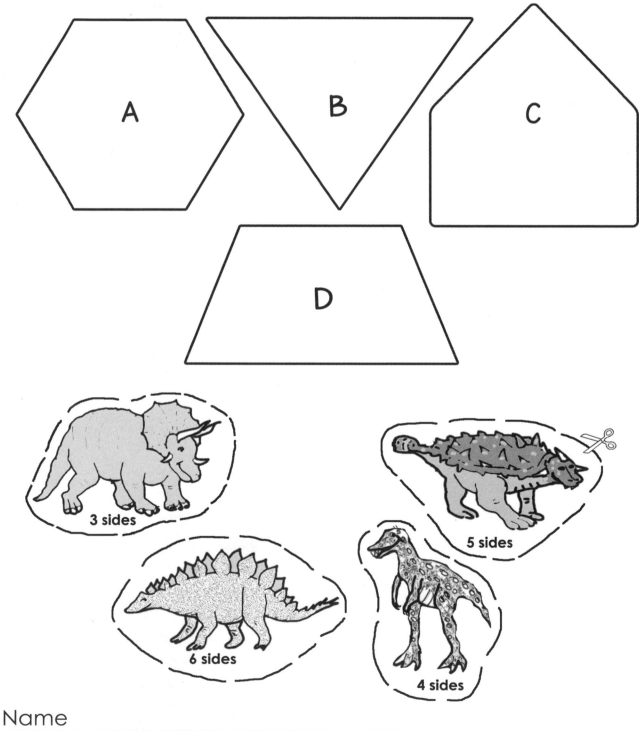

Name _____

2D or 3D?

This is a **2D** shape. It is flat.

This is a **3D** shape. It is solid.

Label each shape below as 2D or 3D.

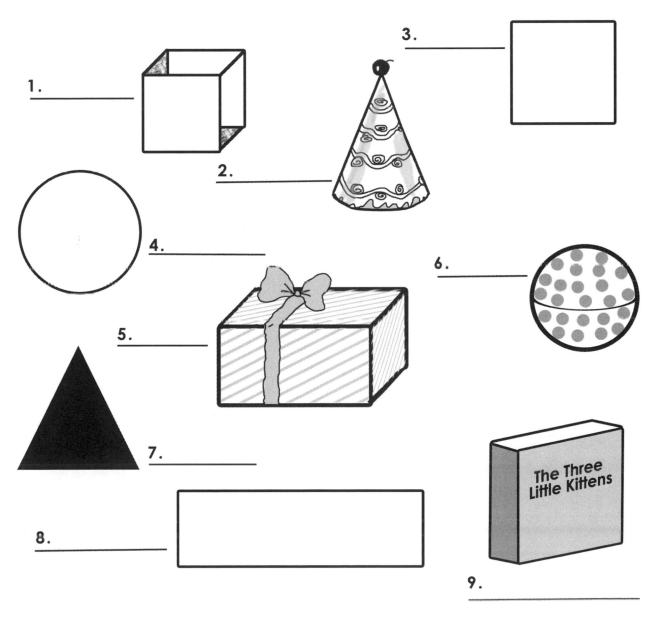

3. _____

1. _____

2. _____

4. _____

6. _____

5. _____

7. _____

8. _____

The Three Little Kittens

9. _____

Name

Identify 2D and 3D Shapes
Common Core Reinforcement Activities — Kindergarten Math

Draw It!

Draw a shape in each square. You decide what to draw!
It can be 2D or 3D.

1	2
3	4

Name

Connect the Dots

Connect the dots to see shapes. Start with number 1.

1. What shapes do you see?

2. Is the whole completed shape you drew 2D or 3D?

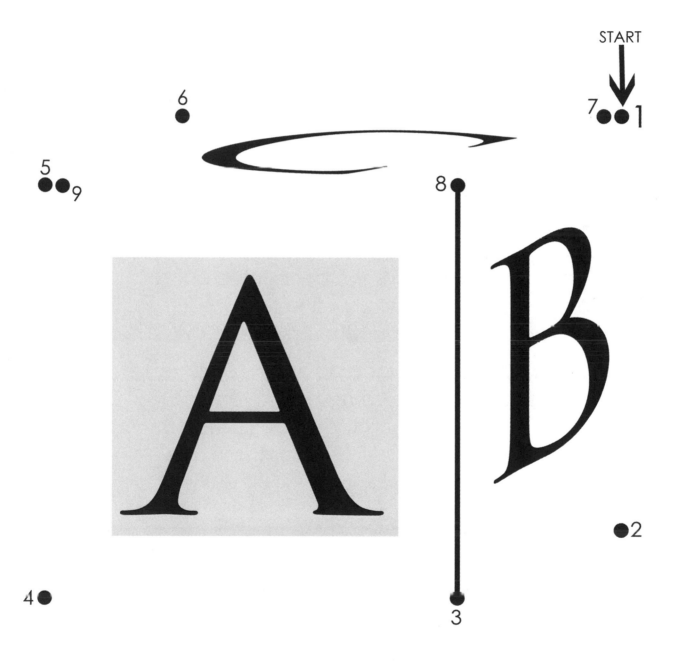

Four Shape Games

Materials: *Shapes for Games cards (pages 127-129)*

To the teacher: Teach students these four shape games to practice identifying shapes and describing their attributes. Mix cards from the three pages. Continue playing each game long enough to provide repeated practice in working with the shapes, giving each player an equal number of turns.

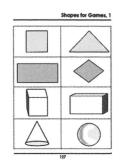

Game 1—A player draws a card from facedown cards and counts the sides of the shape on the card. Others in the group check the count. If it is correct, the card is awarded to the first counter. If the count is not correct, the card is returned to the bottom of the pile. Repeat with other players.

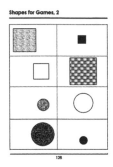

Game 2—A player draws a card from the stack of cards and names the shape. If the group confirms the name, this player keeps the card. If the name is not correct, the card is returned to the bottom of the pile. Play continues with others taking turns.

Game 3—Arrange cards face down on table. A player chooses two cards, turns them over, and names each shape. If the shapes match, the player takes the cards. If the shapes do not match, the cards are returned to their original positions. The next player takes a turn.

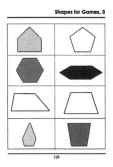

Game 4—A player draws a card from stack of cards and describes the attributes of the shape on the card. Other players try to name the shape.

Sides and Corners

Count the sides. Make a mark on each side as you count it.

Count the corners. Circle the corner as you count it.

Another name for corner is **vertex** (plural, **vertices**).

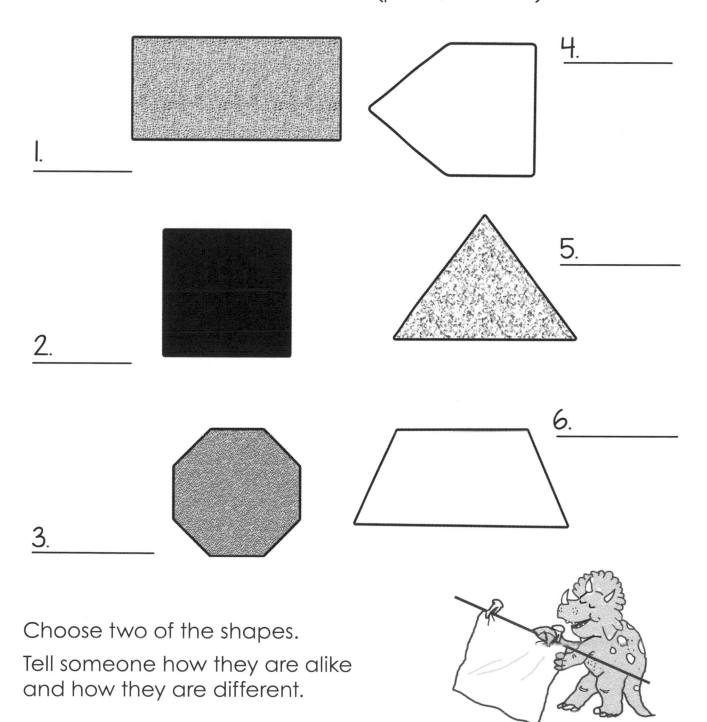

1. _____

2. _____

3. _____

4. _____

5. _____

6. _____

Choose two of the shapes.

Tell someone how they are alike and how they are different.

Name

Analyze and Compare Shapes
Common Core Reinforcement Activities — Kindergarten Math

Make the Shapes

To the teacher: Invite children to use geoboards and rubber bands to make shapes before doing this pencil-paper activity.

Make shapes by connecting dots. Can you make a square? a rectangle? a hexagon? an octagon?

Tell about the shapes you made. Choose two and tell about how they are alike and different.

Name

Faces and Corners

Count the faces. Count the corners. Can you see them all?

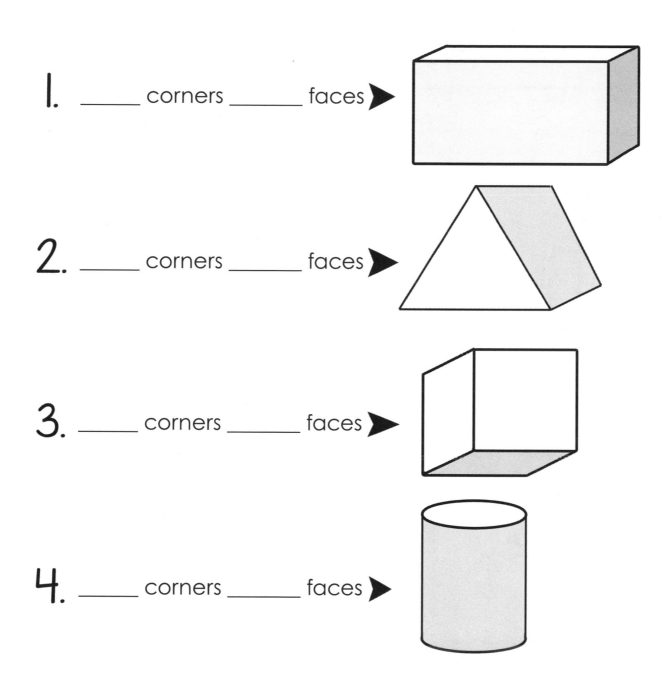

1. _____ corners _____ faces ▶

2. _____ corners _____ faces ▶

3. _____ corners _____ faces ▶

4. _____ corners _____ faces ▶

Choose two of the shapes. Tell someone how they are alike and how they are different.

Name

Analyze and Compare Shapes
Common Core Reinforcement Activities — Kindergarten Math

Shapes All Around Me

Match the drawing of the shape with the object in the photo that has the same shape. Tell about how they are alike.

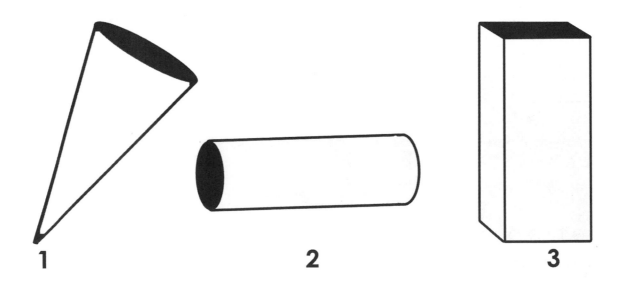

Name

Seeing Shapes in Objects

Look at the shape in each row. Draw one familiar object that has the same shape.

1.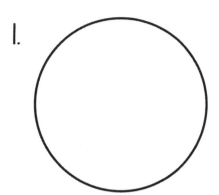

Draw your object here.

2.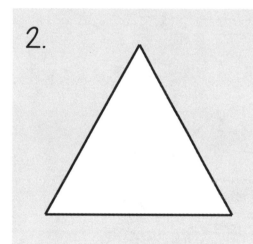

Draw your object here.

3.

Draw your object here.

Tell about how the objects are like the shapes.

Name _____

Draw Familiar Shapes
Common Core Reinforcement Activities — Kindergarten Math

Make New Shapes

Materials: *Small Shapes (page 130)*

Use the small shapes to make the bigger shapes.

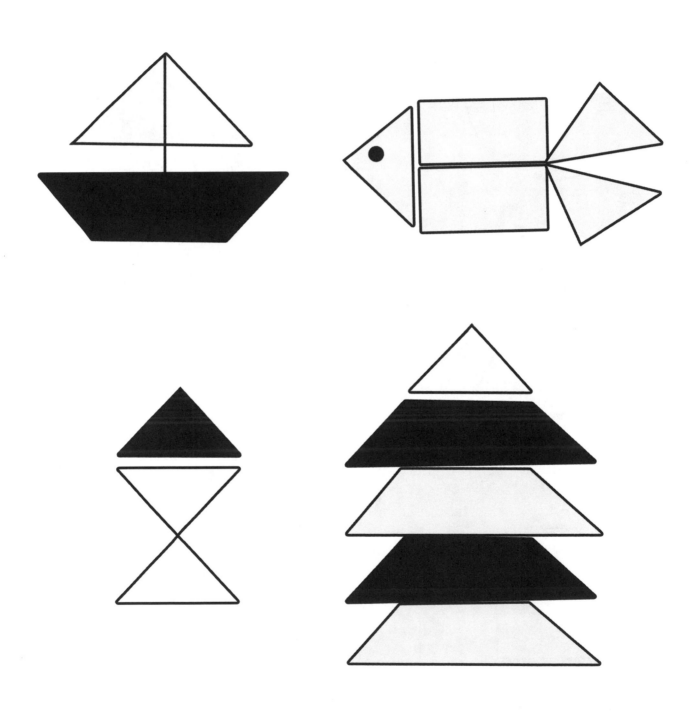

Make Pictures with Shapes

Materials: *Small Shapes (page 130)*

Use small shapes to make a house and a dinosaur.

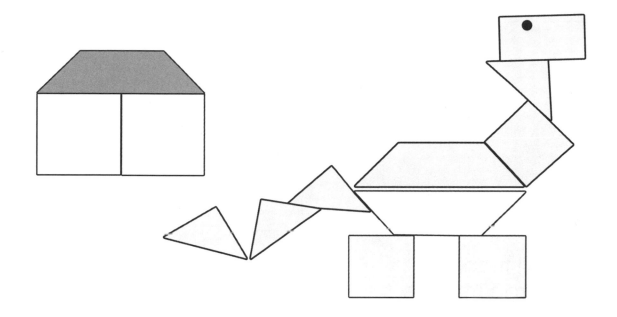

Use the shapes to make a picture of your own here.
Draw around the shapes to show your picture.

Name

Combine Shapes to Form Larger Shapes
Common Core Reinforcement Activities — Kindergarten Math

Build Shapes with Triangles

Materials: *triangles from the Small Shapes collection (page 130)*

To the teacher: A quick photo snapped on a digital camera is a great way to record each of these shapes.

Use 2 small triangles.
Make a large triangle.

Use 4 small triangles.
Make a rectangle.

Use 6 small triangles.
Make a hexagon.

Use 8 small triangles.
Make a square.

Use triangles to make another shape. Draw the new shape on the back of this page.

Name

REPRODUCIBLE MANIPULATIVES AND AIDS

Contents

Dinosaur Counters

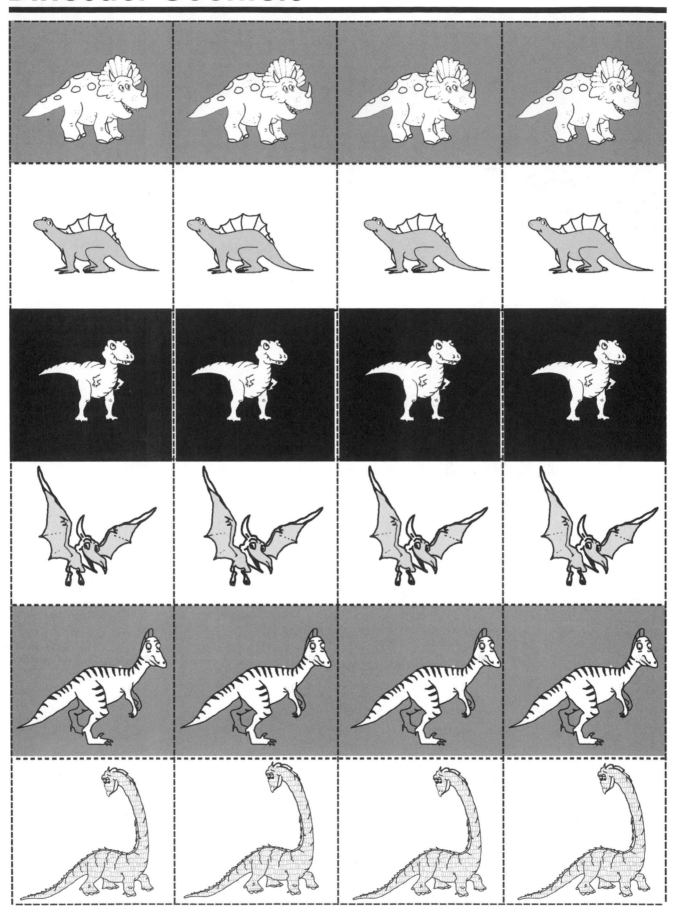

Footprint Counters

Fossil Counters

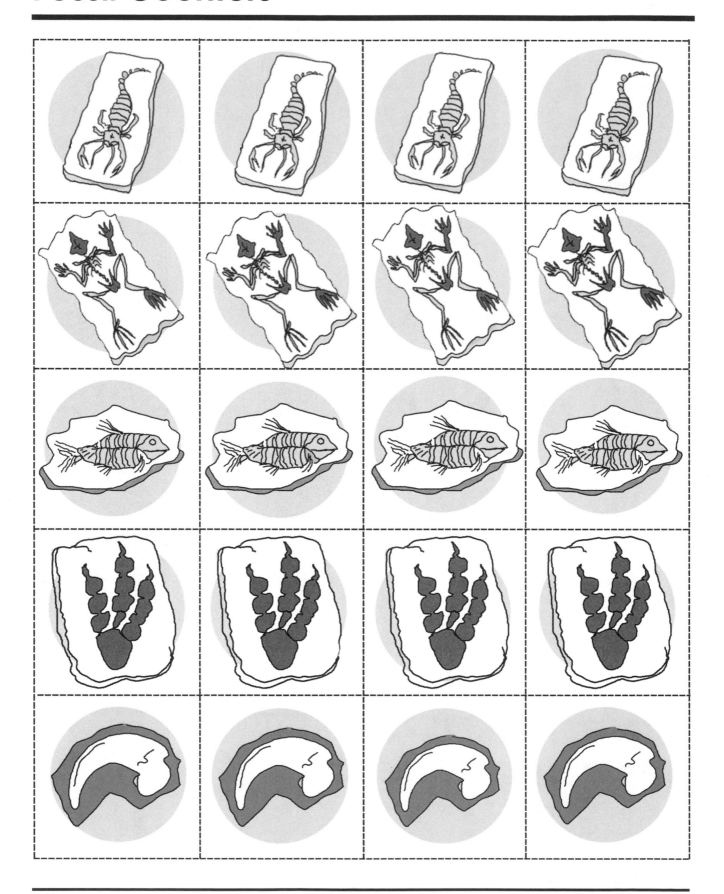

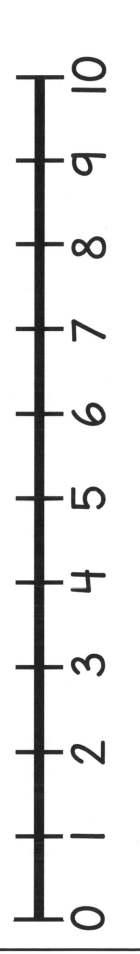

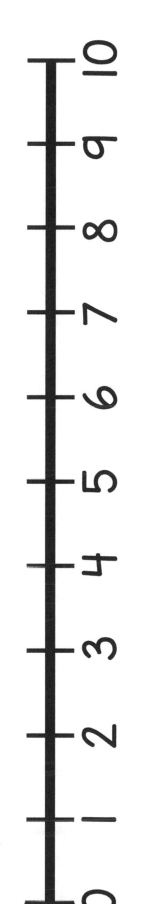

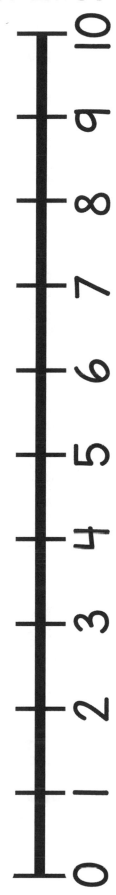

Common Core Reinforcement Activities — Kindergarten Math

Dinosaur Number Cards 0-3

0

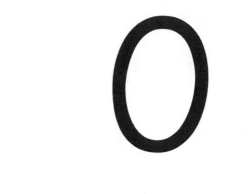

Hold the card with the dinosaur at the bottom.

1

Hold the card with the dinosaur at the bottom.

2

Hold the card with the dinosaur at the bottom.

3

Hold the card with the dinosaur at the bottom.

4

Hold the card with the dinosaur at the bottom.

5

Hold the card with the dinosaur at the bottom.

6

Hold the card with the dinosaur at the bottom.

7

Hold the card with the dinosaur at the bottom.

Dinosaur Number Cards 8-11

8

Hold the card with the dinosaur at the bottom.

9

Hold the card with the dinosaur at the bottom.

10

Hold the card with the dinosaur at the bottom.

11

Hold the card with the dinosaur at the bottom.

Swamp Mat

Common Core Reinforcement Activities — Kindergarten Math

Dinosaur Cutouts for Story Problems, 1

Dinosaur Cutouts for Story Problems, 2

Common Core Reinforcement Activities — Kindergarten Math

Dinosaur Habitat

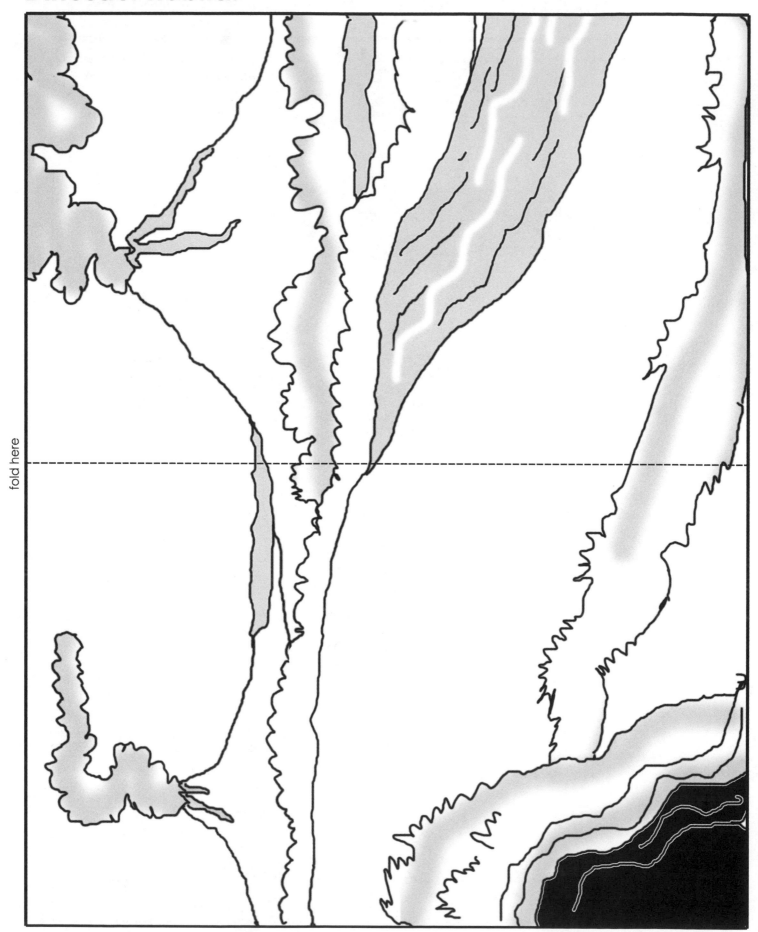

fold here

Teen Number Cards

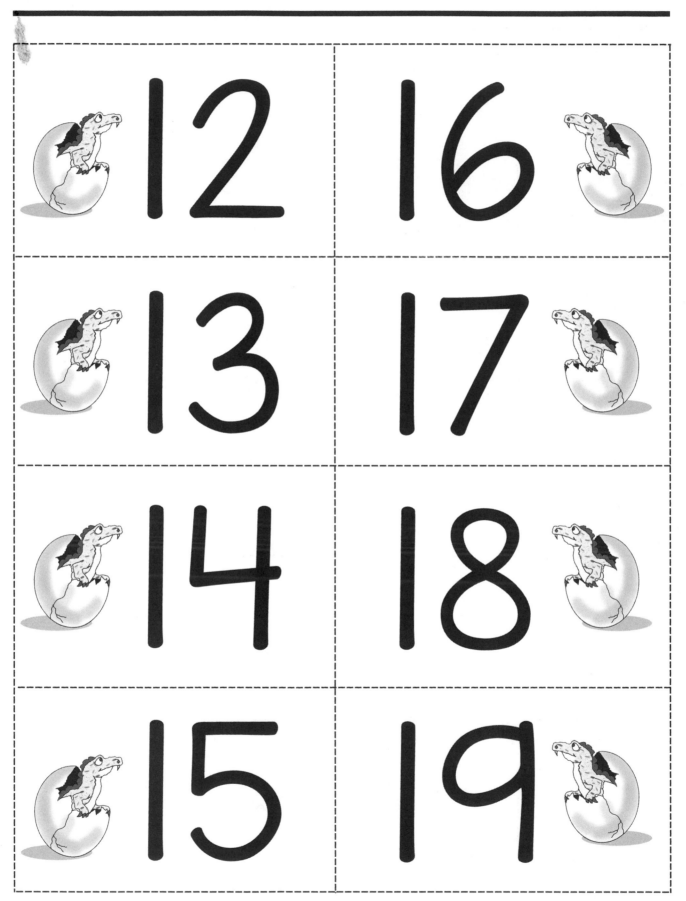

Dinosaurs for Sorting, 1

Brachiosaurus

could reach its head as high as two double-decker buses

longer front legs than back legs

long neck, small head, and relatively short tail

ate 250–500 pounds (113-227 kg) of plants a day

walked on four legs

plant eater (herbivore)

75 feet (23 m) long

85 tons (77 metric tons)

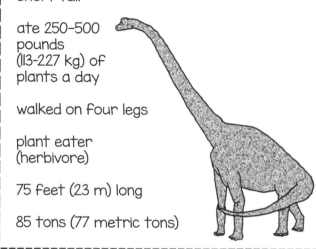

Diplodocus

long thin neck and long thin tail—one of the longest animals to have lived on Earth

had peg-like teeth for stripping soft plants, but couldn't chew

swallowed stones to help grind the plant material in its stomach

walked on four legs

plant eater (herbivore)

90 feet (27 m) long

11 tons (10 metric tons)

Triceratops

three horns on face (two brow horns and a nose horn)

sharp, curved beak and powerful jaws

huge bony frill around neck

400–800 teeth

walked on four legs

plant eater (herbivore)

25 feet (2.1 m) long

8 tons (7.3 metric tons)

Apatosaurus

one of the largest animals ever to have walked on Earth

long whip-like tail balanced long neck

one blunt claw on each foreleg

walked on four legs

plant eater (herbivore)

75 feet (23 m) long

33 tons (30 metric tons)

Common Core Reinforcement Activities — Kindergarten Math

Dinosaurs for Sorting, 2

Bactrosaurus

one of the duck-billed dinosaurs

front of head had a toothless snout resembling a duck's bill

rows of self-sharpening teeth in the back of the mouth

a line of spine-like projections along its back and tail

walked on two legs

plant eater (herbivore)

25 feet (7.6 m) long

3 tons (2.7 metric tons)

Compsognathus

small with tapered snout and small, sharp teeth

short forelimbs; two long, thin back legs

hollow bones and a flexible neck

fast and agile

walked on two legs

meat eater (carnivore)

2 1/2 feet (0.8 m) long

6.5 pounds (3 kg)

Oviraptor

sharp, toothless beak

fast runner

birdlike features

cared for its eggs

walked on two legs

meat eater (carnivore) and, maybe, plant eater (herbivore)

6 1/2 feet (2 m) long

75 pounds (34 kg)

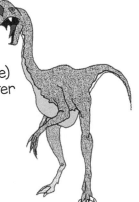

Velociraptor

sharp claws on rear feet

may have hunted together in packs

may have had feathers

walked on two legs

meat eater (carnivorous)

6 feet (1.8 m) long

33 pounds (15 kg)

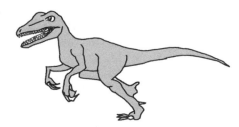

Iguanodon

one of the first dinosaurs discovered (1822)

thin skull and a long tail

long spikes on thumbs

three middle fingers of hands webbed together

walked on two legs and four legs

plant eater (herbivore)

30 feet (9 m) long

4 tons (3.6 metric tons)

Spinosaurus

among the largest meat-eating dinosaurs

distinctive "sail" on back (long spines covered in skin)

6-foot (2-m) head with narrow snout and straight, knife-like teeth

probably killed its prey by shaking it

walked on two legs

meat eater (carnivore)

41–47 feet (12.6–14.3 m) long

12.9 tons (11.7 metric tons)

Allosaurus

three-fingered hands with sharp claws

two bony lumps in front of its eyes

hind feet had three toes pointing forward and one toe pointing backward

walked on two legs

meat eater (carnivore)

up to 36 feet (11 m) long

2 tons (1.8 metric tons)

Ankylosaurus

huge plates of body armor to protect itself

large body with massive tail club could swing 100 pound (45 kg) club and shatter the legs of rivals

had beak and small teeth

walked on four legs

plant eater (herbivore)

25 feet (7.6 m) long

4 tons (3.6 metric tons)

Common Core Reinforcement Activities — Kindergarten Math

Dinosaurs for Sorting, 4

Tyrannosaurus Rex
(T-rex)

many long, sharp, serrated teeth

powerful tail balanced weight of body and giant head

small, powerful two-fingered arms

may have been a scavenger, eating bodies of dead animals, as well as a hunter

average lifespan of up to 30 years

walked on two legs

meat eater (carnivore)

40 feet (12 m) long

7 tons
(6.3 metric tons)

Stegosaurus

rows of bony plates along back and spikes on tail

front legs less than half as long as back legs

tail spikes could be 3 feet (90 cm) long

small, narrow head with beak at front and teeth farther back

walked on four legs

plant eater (herbivore)

30 feet (9 m) long

5 tons
(4.5 metric tons)

Pteranodon

a large flying toothless reptile, not a dinosaur

wings covered by a stretchy membrane

hollow bones, crest on head, and almost no tail

flew; walked clumsily on two feet

meat eater (carnivore)

wingspan of
36–39 feet
(7.8–10 m)

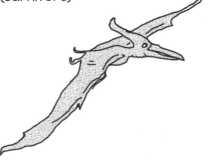

Wannanosaurus

one of smallest dinosaurs

thick skull

primitive member of the bonehead dinosaurs

walked on two legs

plant eater (herbivore), but may have eaten meat, too

3 feet (1 m) long

Shapes to Compare

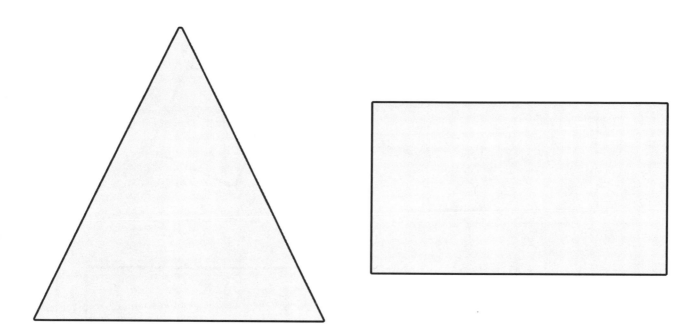

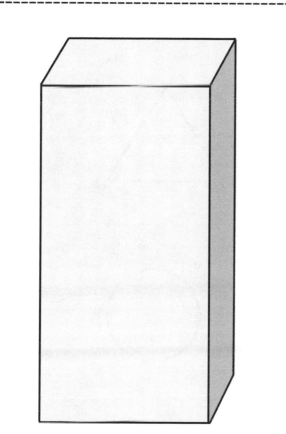

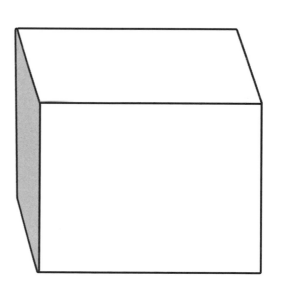

Common Core Reinforcement Activities — Kindergarten Math

Shapes for Sorting

square	rectangle	triangle	circle

Shapes for Games, 1

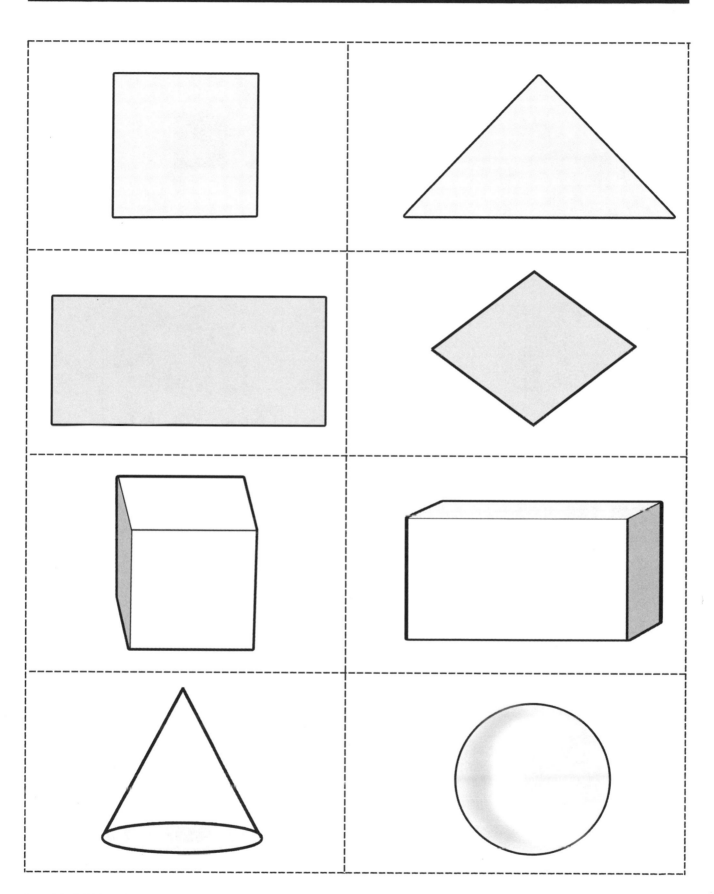

Common Core Reinforcement Activities — Kindergarten Math

Shapes for Games, 2

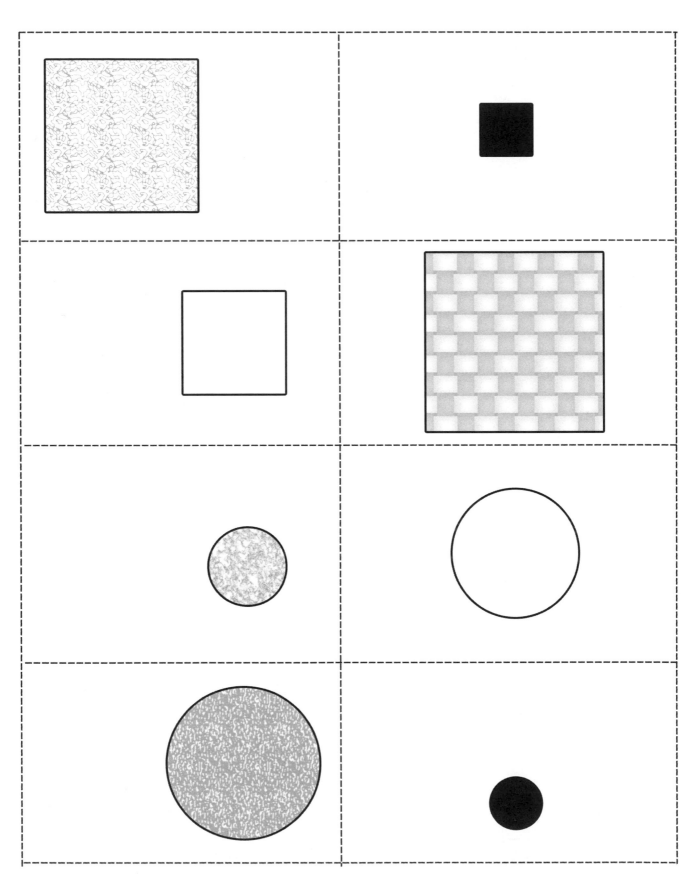

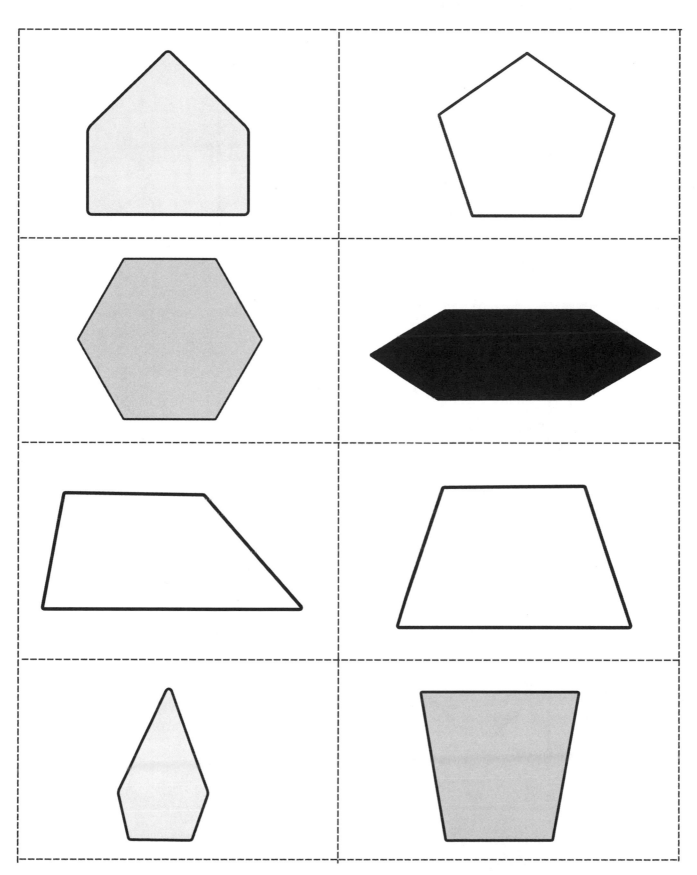

129

Common Core Reinforcement Activities — Kindergarten Math

Small Shapes

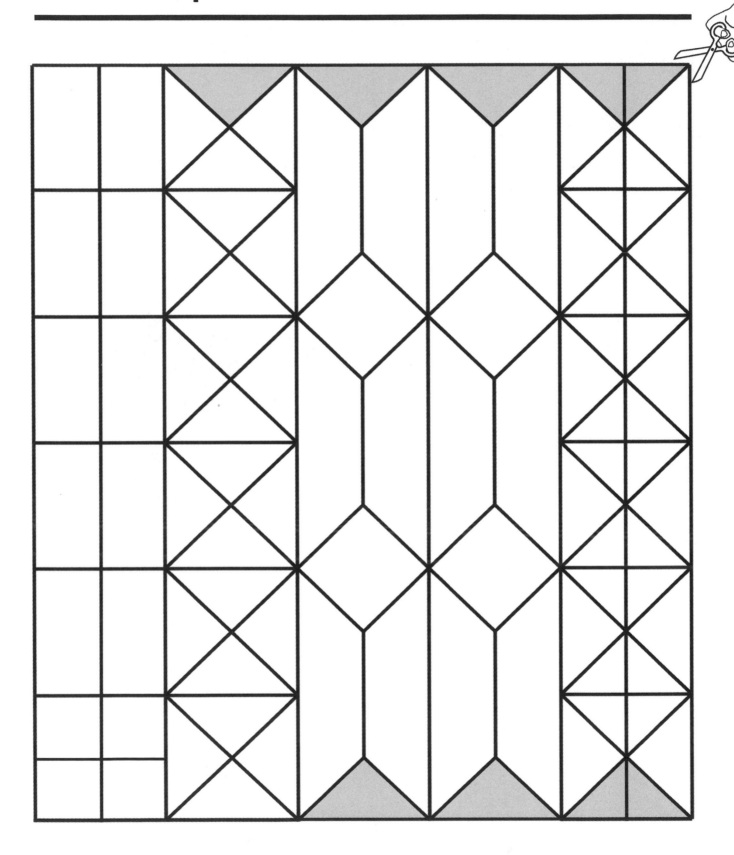

ASSESSMENT AND ANSWER KEYS

Notes on Assessment:

When assessing kindergarten students, the use of a range of assessment methods provides a detailed account of the child's learning and development. Observation gives immediate information about how and what students are learning. Provide samples of students' work as evidence of their learning and development.

Assessment tasks: Use the tasks on pages 132-135 for formative or summative assessment of individual kindergarten math standards. The task descriptions are prompts for you to use along with counters, number cards, or other materials that enable the student to show understanding of and ability with the standard. Where writing is necessary, the student can write on a small whiteboard or a blank piece of paper.

Cumulative Assessment: More traditional tests, like the cumulative assessment on pages 137-141, provide additional insight into a student's ability to apply mathematical strategies to solve problems. Give the test to individuals or small groups. Read the questions to students and observe them as they solve the problems.

Contents

Math Assessment Tasks

Make a copy of page 136 for each student. Use these copies to keep records of students' progress on assessment tasks.

Counting and Cardinality

Standard	Say to the student:
K.CC.A.1	Count as far as you can. Start with 1.
K.CC.A.2	Count again. This time start with 12. (Stop student at 30.)
	Try again, this time start with 46. (Stop student at 65.)

K.CC.A.3   ***Materials:*** *paper and pencil or whiteboard and marker*

Write the number 3. Write the number 14.

Write the number 7. Write the number 16.

Write the number 5.

K.CC.B.4   ***Materials:*** *Dinosaur Counters (page 108)*

(Lay out four dinosaur counters.) Ask: How many are there?

(Mix up the counters.) Ask: How many are there?

(Invite student to take a small handful of counters and count them.) Ask: How many are there?

(Mix up the counters.) Ask: How many are there?

K.CC.B.5   ***Materials:*** *Dinosaur Counters (page 108)*

For each action below, ask: How many dinosaurs are there?

- (Show 7 dinosaurs in a scattered configuration.)
- (Show 13 dinosaurs in a straight horizontal line.)
- (Show 18 dinosaurs in a straight vertical line.)

K.CC.C.6   ***Materials:*** *Dinosaur Counters (page 108)*

(Show a group of four counters and a group of six counters.) Ask: Is the first group greater than, less than, or equal to the second group?

(Show two groups of seven counters.) Ask: Is the first group greater than, less than, or equal to the second group?

(Show a group of three counters and a group of five counters.) Ask: Is the first group greater than, less than, or equal to the second group?

Standard	Say to the student:
K.CC.C.7	**Materials:** *Number Cards 8, 3, 1, 2, 5, 5 (pages 112-114)*

(Show two cards.) Ask: Is the first numeral greater than, less than, or equal to the second numeral?

8	3
1	2
5	5

Operations and Algebraic Thinking

Standard	Say to the student:
K.OA.A.1	**Materials:** *counters (pages 108-110); paper and pencil*

(Read each problem to the student. Invite her or him to use counters, fingers, drawings, or numbers to solve it.)

- There were two dinosaurs by the rock. Two more dinosaurs came. How many dinosaurs are there now?

- One man found two bones, and another man found six bones. How many bones did they find in all?

- Four Pteranodons landed on the branch. Three of them flew away. How many are there now?

- Seven giant fish swam in the sea. Five of them swam away. How many are there now?

| K.OA.A.2 | **Materials:** *counters (pages 108-110); paper and pencil* |

(Read each problem to the student. Invite her or him to use counters, fingers, drawings, or numbers to solve it.)

- Three dinosaurs are in the lake. Four more wade in. How many dinosaurs are in the lake now?

- Four Long-necks stretched their heads above the trees. One bends his head down to take a drink. How many Long-necks are still looking around?

- Five Triceratops plod into the clearing. One turns around and goes back into the trees. How many Triceratops are in the clearing?

- There were nine eggs in the dinosaur's next. Three of the eggs hatch. How many unhatched eggs are left?

Standard	Say to the student:
K.OA.A.3	***Materials:*** *ten counters (pages 108-110); paper and pencil*
	Show how to make ten with two groups.
	Show a second way to make ten with two groups.
K.OA.A.4	(Write each number for the student to see.)
	Read the number. Tell how many more make ten.
	3 8 1 5 7
K.OA.A.5	(Write each problem for the student to see.)
	Find the answers.

$3 + 1 =$

$2 + 3 =$

$1 + 4 =$

$5 - 2 =$

$3 - 1 =$

$4 - 3 =$

Number and Operations in Base Ten

Standard	Say to the student:
K.NBT.A.1	***Materials:*** *Ten-Frames (page 119); objects; paper and pencil*
	(Show full ten-frame plus six ones.)
	Ask: How many objects are there?
	(Show group of ten in ring plus three outside ring.)
	Ask: How many counters are there?
	(Show 13.)
	(Show 18.)

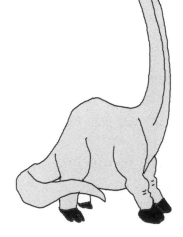

Measurement and Data

Standard	Say to the student:
K.MD.A.1	**Materials:** *picture of Diplodocus (page 80)*
	Tell about the different ways to measure the dinosaur.
K.MD.A.2	**Materials:** *two Dinosaur Cutouts (pages 116-117)*
	Compare the two dinosaurs. Tell which one is taller. Tell which one looks heavier.
K.MD.B.3	**Materials:** *Dinosaurs for Sorting cards (pages 121-124)*
	Sort the dinosaurs into groups with these characteristics.

spikes   no spikes

tails   no tails

Geometry

Standard	Say to the student:
K.G.A.1	**Materials:** *picture of four dinosaurs (page 90)*
	Tell about where the dinosaurs are standing.
K.G.A.2	**Materials:** *Shapes for Sorting (page 126)*
	Name the shapes.
K.G.A.3	**Materials:** *copy of shapes on page 96*
	Sort the 2D and 3D shapes.
K.G.B.4	**Materials:** *Shapes to Compare (page 125)*
	Tell about how the two shapes are alike and different.
K.G.B.5	**Materials:** *paper and pencil or whiteboard and marker*
	Draw a circle.
	Draw a triangle.
K.G.B.6	**Materials:** *shapes from page of Small Shapes (page 130)*
	Combine some small shapes to make a big shape.

Assessment Tasks Progress Record

Student's Name _____

Enter date standard is assessed and checkmark in relevant column.

Counting and Cardinality

Date	Standard	Fluent and Confident	Independent	With Support	Developing	Not Yet	Notes
	K.CC.A.1						
	K.CC.A.2						
	K.CC.A.3						
	K.CC.A.4						
	K.CC.B.5						
	K.CC.C.6						
	K.CC.C.7						

Operations and Algebraic Thinking

Date	Standard	Fluent and Confident	Independent	With Support	Developing	Not Yet	Notes
	K.OA.A.1						
	K.OA.A.2						
	K.OA.A.3						
	K.OA.A.4						
	K.OA.A.5						

Number and Operations in Base Ten

Date	Standard	Fluent and Confident	Independent	With Support	Developing	Not Yet	Notes
	K.NBT.A.1						

Measurement and Data

Date	Standard	Fluent and Confident	Independent	With Support	Developing	Not Yet	Notes
	K.MD.A.1						
	K.MD.A.2						
	K.MD.B.3						

Geometry

Date	Standard	Fluent and Confident	Independent	With Support	Developing	Not Yet	Notes
	K.G.A.1						
	K.G.A.2						
	K.G.A.3						
	K.G.B.4						
	K.G.B.5						
	K.G.B.6						

Cumulative Math Assessment

To the teacher: Before giving out the printed assessment, interview individual students with the following prompts. Listen to the counting and make notes about accuracy.

1. Start with 18 and count until I stop you.

2. Count by tens to 100.

---

3. Write numbers from 0 to 20.

4. How many eggs in the dinosaur's nest?

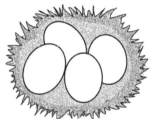

5. Touch and count to tell how many teeth.

6. Write the number to tell how many:

A.

B.

C.

Name

Date:

Cumulative Math Assessment
Common Core Reinforcement Activities — Kindergarten Math

For 7 – 11, circle the words that are correct.

7.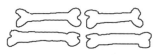

is less than
is more than
is equal to

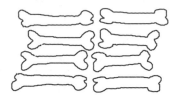

8.

is less than
is more than
is equal to

9. 9 **is less than** 3
is more than
is equal to

10. 11 **is less than** 18
is more than
is equal to

11.   zero **is less than** 0
is more than
is equal to

12. Draw pictures to show the answer.

3 bones + 5 bones =

13. Draw on the dinosaur to show the answer.

7 spikes + 2 spikes =

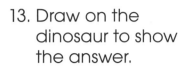

Solve the problems.

14. Diplodocus ate two leaves off one tree and one leaf off another tree. How many leaves did it eat in all?

15. T-rex catches three, and then he catches two more. How many did T-rex catch?

16. Draw two sets of dinosaur eggs. There should be ten dinosaur eggs in all.

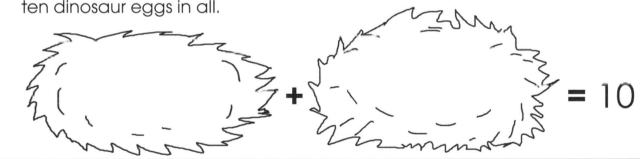

17. How many more are needed to make ten? Write the number.

A. _____ + _____ = 10

B. _____ + _____ = 10

18. Solve the problems.

A. 3 + 2 = ☐

C. 1 + 3 = ☐

E. 0 + 2 = ☐

B. 4 − 1 = ☐

D. 5 − 4 = ☐

F. 3 − 3 = ☐

19. Tell how many items.

A. 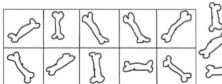 ☐

B. 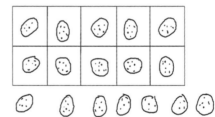 ☐

20. Tell how many items.

A.  ☐

B. ☐

21. Circle the tallest dinosaur.

A.   B.   C.

22. Circle the dinosaurs that walk on two legs.

A.   B.   C.   D.   E.

23. Color the dinosaur that is **beside** the rock. Put an X on the dinosaur that is right **in front of** the tree. Circle the dinosaur that is **behind** the tree.

24. Draw a line to match the shape to its name.

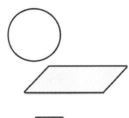

square
triangle
circle
rectangle

25. Circle the label that names the kind of shape.

A.
2D   3D

B.
2D   3D

C.
2D   3D

26. Draw an animal made out of shapes. Tell about the shapes you used.

Cumulative Math Assessment
Answer Key

1. and 2. Make notes about student's counting accuracy.
3. Make notes about how student writes numbers.
4. 4
5. 9
6. A. 8; B. 0; C. 13
7. is less than
8. is more than
9. is more than
10. is less than
11. is equal to
12. Look for student drawing of 8 bones.
13. Look for student drawing of 9 spikes on dinosaur.
14. 3
15. 5

16. Look for drawing of 2 sets that equal ten eggs.
17. A. 7; B. 4
18. A. 5; B. 3; C. 4; D. 1; E. 2; F. 0
19. A. 8; B. 10
20. A. 13; B. 17
21. B
22. B and E
23. Check pictures to see that correct dinosaurs are colored, X'd, and circled.
24. Check to see that student has matched shapes and names accurately.
25. A. 3D; B. 2D; C. 3D
26. Observe student drawings and listen to their explanations.

Activities Answer Key

Counting and Cardinality (pages 18-42)

pages 18, 19, 20, 21, and 22
Listen for counting accuracy.

page 23
Next numbers 9; 13; 18; 10; 16; 20

page 24
Next numbers 35; 74; 49; 52; 70; 86

page 25
Check for accuracy of tracing, writing, and counting.

pages 26 and 27
Observe to gauge skill at perceiving number accurately without counting.

pages 28 and 29
Observe accuracy of counting and number recognition.

page 30
1. 3
2. 5
3. 2
4. 0

page 31
1. 1
2. 6
3. 2
4. 3
5. Check drawings for one nest with five eggs.

page 32
1. 6
2. 4
3. 3
4. 1
5. 5
6. 2
Check arrangements to see that students have matched the patterns.

page 33
Observe to gauge skill at counting and writing numbers.

page 34
1. 2
2. 4
3. 1
4. Answers will vary. Check for accuracy.
5. Review coloring for accuracy.

page 35
1. 10
2. 4
3. 5
4. Answers will vary. Check for accuracy.
5. Check drawings for five stripes.

page 36
1. 17
2. 4

3. 6
4. 2
5. Listen for accuracy as students count one another's dinosaurs.

page 37
Observe students for counting accuracy.

pages 38 and 39
Observe students for counting and comparison accuracy.

page 40
A. 8; B. 7; C. 3; D. 9; E. 8; F. 5; G. 9; H. 7; I. 9; J. 10; Listen to student explanations for reasonable arguments.

pages 41-42
Observe for counting and comparison accuracy.

Operations and Algebraic Thinking (pages 44-68)

pages 44 and 45
Observe and listen as students tell and act out math stories.

page 46
1. 4
2. 4
3. 5
4. 5
5. 4
6. 4
7. 5
8. 3

page 47
Observe and listen as students draw and tell stories.

page 48
Look for story sequences that tell an addition or subtraction story.

page 49
1. 3
2. 2
3. Review students' stories for accuracy.

page 50
Observe and listen as students tell and show math stories.
1. 4
2. 4
3. 3
4. 5

page 51
1. 8
2. 7
3. 6
4. 8

page 52
Observe and listen as students tell and show math stories.
1. 2
2. 2
3. Answers will vary.

page 53
1. 5
2. 6
3. 7
4. 0
5. 6

page 54
1. 3
2. 4
3. 6
4. 5
5. 1

page 55
Review pictures to see how student used them to find solve the problem.
1. 2, subtract
2. 10; add
3. 6; add
4. 4; subtract

page 56
Review pictures and listen to explanations about student's thinking.
1. 2; 1
2. 2; 1

page 57
Observe and listen as students show stories and explain their ideas for changing the stories.

1. 3; 2
2. 4; 3
3. 6; 2

page 58
Review drawings and listen to student's solutions.

page 59
Review drawings and listen to student's solutions. Look for:
1. 2 yellow
2. 8 yellow
3. 4 yellow
4. 9 yellow
5. 7 yellow
6. 5 yellow

page 60
1. 7
2. 1
3. 5
4. 8
5. 3
6. 6

page 61
Observe players to check accuracy of problems.

page 62
Observe players as they play the game; watch for accuracy of operations.

page 63
Observe play and review record sheets.

page 64
1. 5
2. 5

3. 5
4. 5
5. 5
Observe play and review record sheets.

page 65
1. 5
2. 2
3. 4
4. 1
5. 3
6. 0
Observe use of the five-frame.

page 66
1. 2
2. 2
3. 1
4. 2
5. 2
6. 0
Observe use of the five-frame.

page 67
1. 2
2. 2
3. 1
4. 2
5. 2
6. 2
7. 0
8. 0
Observe use of the five-frame.

page 68
Observe and review student's original problems for accuracy in adding and subtracting within five.

Number and Operations in Base Ten (pages 70-78)

page 70
Observe and listen to student's explanations.
1. 10
2. 10; Answers to second question will vary.
3. 14
4. 12
5. 13

pages 71, 72, 73, and 74
Observe for accuracy as student builds and shows numbers.

page 75
1. D
2. F
3. B
4. C

5. A
6. E

page 76
Review drawings for accuracy.

page 77
Review drawings to see that they match numbers.

page 78
Review drawings to see that they match numbers.

Measurement and Data (pages 80-88)

page 80

Listen for reasonable descriptions and comparisons of attributes.

pages 81 and 82

Measurements will vary depending on units used. Listen to students' reasoning about the weights of the dinosaur.

pages 83 and 84

Listen for reasonable descriptions and comparisons of attributes.

page 85

Look for dinosaurs correctly sorted. Three walked on two legs.

page 86

Look for dinosaurs correctly sorted.

page 87

C

page 88

B

Geometry (pages 90-106)

pages 90-91

Observe and listen to student and student's work for accurate position identification.

page 92

Look for dinosaurs correctly placed in shapes. Note: Some students may note that a square is a rectangle, so the dinosaur with the "square" sign could be in either spot.

page 93

Observe student sorting and listen to the explanations.

page 94

A. 6 sides; hexagon
B. 3 sides; triangle
C. 5 sides; pentagon
D. 4 sides; trapezoid

page 95

1. 3D
2. 3D
3. 2D
4. 2D
5. 3D
6. 3D
7. 2D
8. 2D
9. 3D

page 96

Review student drawings and listen to their explanations.

page 97

Students may report seeing a square and 2 parallelograms. The completed shape is 3D.

page 98

Observe game play and listen for accurate naming, analysis, and comparison of shapes.

page 99

1. 4 sides, 4 corners
2. 4 sides, 4 corners
3. 8 sides, 8 corners
4. 5 sides, 5 corners
5. 3 sides, 3 corners
6. 4 sides, 4 corners
   On the final task, listen to student explanations for accuracy and reasonableness.

page 100

Review student drawings and listen to their explanations for accuracy and reasonableness.

page 101

1. 8 corners, 6 faces
2. 6 corners, 5 faces
3. 8 corners, 6 faces
4. 0 corners, 3 faces
   On the final task, listen to student explanations for accuracy and reasonableness. They will not be able to see all faces and corners.

page 102

1. center picture
2. right-hand picture
3. left-hand picture
   Listen to student explanations for accuracy and reasonableness.

page 103

Observe student drawings and listen to the explanations for accuracy and reasonableness.

pages 104, 105, and 106

Review student work for accuracy.